THE ULTIMATE GUIDE TO COLLEGE TRANSFER

THE ULTIMATE GUIDE TO COLLEGE TRANSFER

From Surviving to Thriving

Lucia D. Tyler and Susan E. Henninger

ROWMAN & LITTLEFIELD
Lanham • Boulder • New York • London

Published by Rowman & Littlefield
A wholly owned subsidiary of The Rowman & Littlefield Publishing Group, Inc.
4501 Forbes Boulevard, Suite 200, Lanham, Maryland 20706
www.rowman.com

Unit A, Whitacre Mews, 26-34 Stannary Street, London SE11 4AB

British Library Cataloguing in Publication Information Available

Library of Congress Cataloging-in-Publication Data Available

ISBN: 978-1-4758-2686-9 (cloth : alk. paper)
ISBN: 978-1-4758-2689-0 (electronic)

♾ ™ The paper used in this publication meets the minimum requirements of American National Standard for Information Sciences—Permanence of Paper for Printed Library Materials, ANSI/NISO Z39.48-1992.

Printed in the United States of America

CONTENTS

ACKNOWLEDGMENTS

SUSAN'S ACKNOWLEDGMENTS

Writing this book has been a fascinating journey for me. Talking with college students and their parents, it has amazed me how much, and yet how little, the transfer process and the emotions that accompany it have changed since I transferred between four-year colleges in the 1980s. Having access to a book like this would have definitely made my college transfer a lot easier!

The Ultimate Guide to College Transfer would not have been possible without the help of the following people who reached out to their friends, relatives, professional connections, and perfect strangers to help me find students and parents from all over the world to interview. Thanks to Phil Aguglia, Karen Bartishevich, Melissa Bush, Calvin Henninger, Neil Henninger, Ray Henninger, Russell Henninger, Jeanne Hobbie, Kristi Lekies, Faith Meckley, Ginny Miller, Daryl Perlo, Dominique Russell, Ann Silverthorne, Greg and Sharon Spinos, Cathy Thomas, and Arick Wong. Help a Reporter Out (HARO) also netted me several excellent interviews.

I have the best readers in the world! They were honest (sometimes too honest!) and insightful and their comments and feedback were invaluable. My endless appreciation goes out to Melissa Bush, Judi Galusha, Julie Gray, Calvin Henninger, Ray Henninger, Carla Rose, Tammy Tuttobene, and Leonard Winslow for giving so generously of their time and expertise.

Most of all, I want to thank all of the transfer students, parents of transfer students, and higher education professionals I spoke with for sharing their experiences (positive and not so positive) in order to help others learn everything there is to know about college transfer. You know who you are and I'm sure your words will resonate with everyone who reads them!

LUCIA'S ACKNOWLEDGMENTS

The idea for this book first came to mind when I wanted to use such a resource in my own practice as I was helping transfer students several years ago. I gratefully acknowledge my co-author Susan Henninger for helping to make it a reality.

I could not have persevered in this project without the help and encouragement of Dr. Steve Antonoff (author and consultant) and Mr. Mark Sklarow (executive director of Independent Educational Consultants Association [IECA]). Imy Wax (author and consultant) was particularly helpful in the early stages of development. I would also like to thank the college consultants who provided ideas and tips. The consultants are Lora Block, Nancy Griesmer, Julie Gross, Shelley Levine, Jeff Levy, Catherine Marrs, Ann Montgomery, Lori Potts-Dupre, Ann Rossbach, Pam Schachter, and Susan Sykes.

I would like to acknowledge the college professionals who gave generously of their time and expertise. These generous people are Hank Ewert (Austin College), Katie Greene (Embry-Riddle University), Professor Robert Howarth (Cornell University), Barnaby Knoll (University of Puget Sound and Cornell University), Corie Kohlbach (SUNY-Oswego), Laura Kritikos (DePaul University), Kai Lee (Embry Riddle University), Tracy Mores (University of Wisconsin-Madison), and Dr. Sally Neal (Ithaca College). I am also grateful to Mr. Peter Burford, who gave us valuable insights into the world of book publishing. Special thanks go to our editor, Sarah Jubar, whose skilled and knowledgeable guidance helped us throughout the publishing process.

Finally, I must thank my husband, David, and daughter, Emily, for their help and support.

FOREWORD

I spend many weeks a year visiting college campuses. One important part of campus visits for me is talking to students, as they are the ones who know the school best. Unlike faculty members and administrators, students experience the school as it is, not as it is idealized.

Talking to students who have transferred is illuminating. Some of these students feel they are strangers in a strange land. Many are uninvolved and uninformed. They speak about the difficulty of entering a collegiate environment after others have settled. Students may feel out of touch with academic procedures, student life, or importantly, the traditions that bind students together. Student involvement can be particularly lacking as friendship patterns may have been formed, and social groupings established.

It surprises me that colleges have not done more for transfer students. Some colleges have formal or informal transfer orientation programs. Some combine them with freshmen welcoming programs. Other colleges have no programs at all. It's not surprising that students don't know where to turn for information. Worse, current students can shun the new kids on the block—even without knowing it. After all, friendship patterns have already been made, and some student organizations are already closed.

College planning materials have multiplied in recent years. The number of websites and other resources has grown exponentially. There are general guidebooks and websites. There are specialized guidebooks in areas such as costs, careers, essays, learning disabilities, religious life, and ethnic issues. What's missing? Solid, accurate information intended to help those transferring from one college to the next.

Into this void comes *The Ultimate Guide to College Transfer: From Surviving to Thriving*. It's about time! This book organizes and explains the transfer process. This is a book that's been missing from the college planning literature.

Dr. Lucia Tyler has been a trusted colleague of mine for over a decade. She is a counselor who knows her stuff. She engages with the profession. While she is an expert, she is curious enough to seek the perspectives of colleagues, students, and others. She visits colleges and listens to students. She has worked on a college campus and is aware of how the experience feels to students. Her work as a student mentor gives her a "student friendly" outlook and perspective.

I can't think of a better person to guide you through this process than Dr. Tyler. Her interest in transfer students is both academic and emotional. She cares about young people who struggle to know whether transferring is the right thing to do. She empathizes with students transferring into a new environment and who are uncertain as to how to thrive both academically and socially.

Susan E. Henninger adds another important voice to these pages. She has interviewed and written extensively for both magazines and newspapers on family issues. Student and parent interviews are an important part of this book because these families share the things they wished they would have thought about going into the transfer process. Henninger drew out these former transfers and parents of transfers to get beyond the obvious questions to the more nuanced areas of expectations, disappointments, surprises, and overall cultural experiences.

The use of scenarios throughout the book makes issues real and solutions possible. We learn about important topics such as transfer of credit, the special issues involved with international transfer, how to tell parents and friends that one is transferring, how to use technology to make the transfer process easier, and the value of considering community college and gap year options. Significantly, we're given crucial college transfer timelines.

The Ultimate Guide to College Transfer tackles some thorny issues. For example, we learn how to deal with a roommate spending too much time with a romantic interest. We learn how to navigate the often complex financial issues involved in switching from one college to another.

And while the book is a must-read for those who are contemplating transferring (including their parents and advisors), it is also helpful in solving common college-going issues faced by everyone heading off to college. Here you learn where to turn for reliable information, the proper role of parents, and selecting a college major.

Any life change can be stress-inducing, and transferring colleges is no exception. But following the wise words provided by Tyler and Henninger will make the process less confusing, more manageable, and easier.

Steven R. Antonoff, PhD, CEP
Author of *The College Finder* and *College Match: A Blueprint for Choosing the Best College for You*
December, 2016

INTRODUCTION

It's a fact! According to a 2012 report completed by the National Student Clearinghouse Research Center, approximately one-third of all college students in the United States will transfer between colleges at least once before earning their degree. Despite the large number of transfers occurring annually, there is a noticeable lack of resources (online or print) available for the transfer student.

One confusing point is that colleges don't agree on the definition of a "transfer." Some colleges consider a student a transfer if he or she has taken one class for credit after high school while other colleges require far more credits for transfer status. (For a sample of college policies, see appendix C.) Transfers also come in different varieties, including lateral (four-year college to four-year college or two-year college to two-year college), vertical (two-year college to four-year college), and reverse (four-year college to two-year college).

Parents of a potential transfer student may feel like they are in uncharted waters. There are no guides, no best transfer schools, and no "to do" lists. Years of interviews provide helpful combined data to give families a sense of all of the different transfer types. (People profiled in the first two chapters are composites created from multiple transfer families.)

The transfer stories range from academic transfers, to financially based transfers, to medically necessary transfers. The scenarios in the first two chapters include insights and questions to help families relate to their own situation.

Note: "Parents" are used as a broad term throughout the book and include guardians and other significant adults.

The second part of the book gives the parent the benefit of a community of advice. They have the advantage of experience from multiple families from all different types of transfer situations at their fingertips. Parents of transfers will be able to avoid some rocky problems based on current information. Important issues that families wish they had known more about include credit transfer, major graduation requirements, and policies relating to the Family Education Rights and Privacy Act (FERPA) and the disclosure of information to parents.

They also learn of unexpected costs, tangible and intangible, involved in sending a transfer student far away. The best technology and other resources for use in college transfer are shared by college consultants.

The appendices will present various types of resources including a glossary of terms, transfer-friendly practices, a website resource list, and lists of colleges accepting lots of transfers.

FAMOUS COLLEGE TRANSFERS

Barack Obama, *Forty-Fourth President of the United States*	Occidental College to Columbia University
Warren Buffett, *Financier*	University of Pennsylvania to University of Nebraska
Billy Crystal, *Comedian*	Marshall University to Nassau Community College to New York University
Margaret Mead, *Anthropologist/ Author*	DePauw University to Barnard College
Alice Walker, *Author*	Spelman College to Sarah Lawrence College
Lucy Liu, *Actress*	New York University to University of Michigan
Mitt Romney, *Businessman/ Former Governor*	Stanford University to Brigham Young University

Donald Trump, *Forty-Fifth President of the United States*

Fordham University to University of Pennsylvania

Dian Fossey, *Biologist/Author*

University of California to San Diego State University

Jimmy Carter, *Thirty-Ninth President of the United States*

Georgia Southwestern College to Georgia Institute of Technology to United States Naval Academy

James Lehrer, *Journalist/ Television Anchor*

Victoria College to University of Missouri

I

COMMON TRANSFER SCENARIOS

OVERVIEW

Students who are facing problems with roommates, a college that is a poor academic fit, or financial pressures often become unhappy with their college environment and consider transfer. Unrealistic expectations about college life can confront students with a reality check when they arrive on campus, which may also encourage them to explore transfer.

Sometimes the simple knowledge that the unhappy student has an "escape strategy" can help him or her relax as he or she tries to work out problems (with adult help) at their current college. Other times the situation is severe enough that the student will need to arrange for immediate transfer.

REASON TO TRANSFER: ROOMMATE ISSUES

Sometimes a roommate clash happens right away. Other times it builds up gradually, with misunderstandings and irritations accumulating until the living arrangements become unbearable for the hapless student. Many college freshmen have never shared a room with another person on a daily basis. Putting multiple students with different backgrounds, cherished personal possessions, and college pressures in a room together can result in dramatic confrontations or stony avoidance.

The details may differ, but roommate issues are a very common reason for college transfer. Frustration, discomfort, and chronic fatigue can all lead to significant tension between roommates. This affects every aspect of a student's life, sometimes to the point of causing him or her to investigate transferring to a different university.

It's important for parents to take their teen's concerns about the living situation seriously, even when they seem exaggerated. Moving from home to college is a huge adjustment. It's always better to err on the side of caution in cases like these, especially if the college is far away from the student's hometown.

Parents and students shouldn't assume that administrators will take an authoritarian role in situations involving roommates either. College officials will often suggest that students try to "negotiate" around the behaviors in the room or dormitory or simply ignore the situation, hoping it will resolve itself.

Scenario I: Sexiled!

Nick was a frequent "sexile" at a large state university. His roommate had a steady girlfriend who camped out in their room for weeks at a time. Every time she was there, Nick was forced to shuffle between friends' rooms and the dorm lounges because he didn't feel comfortable around all the sexual activity in his room.

Without a real bed, Nick slept poorly and he was tired most of the time. It was hard to get his homework done too. In his rush to get out of the room as quickly as possible, he often found himself without some of the class materials he needed. He worked on papers and studied for tests in the library, but if it closed before he had completed his work he was out of luck.

Because Nick was naturally quiet, his resident assistant (RA) didn't find out about the roommate problem until there was a late night fire drill and Nick was missing from the room check. By this time, his normally high grades had dropped drastically and his parents knew something serious was going on. When the truth emerged, Nick was so miserable that he had no interest in repairing the situation. He told his parents he had made plans to transfer to another school where he could be guaranteed a single room.

If this situation had been diagnosed and dealt with at an earlier stage, Nick most likely would not have felt the need to transfer to a new college. But by the time the adults discovered just how stressed he was, the point of discussion and compromise had come and gone. Nick was adamant about leaving the school and getting a fresh start somewhere else as quickly as possible.

Parent Perspective

Parental support in the form of concern and suggestions or possibly a talk with his resident assistant or the college administration might have either stopped the behavior or resulted in a room change for their son.

Like many older teens, Nick was reticent about his roommate's sexual behavior until the stress became intolerable for him. When sons reach adolescence, parents may find that, unless they ask exactly the right question, boys can be less than forthcoming with personal information or feelings. A typical conversation could go something like this:

Parent: "How's it going at college?"

Son: "Good."

Parent: "So, everything's going well for you?"

Son: "Yeah."

This type of limited exchange often makes it easy for parents to be "stonewalled" by their child. By the end of the conversation they find themselves no wiser than when it began! It can be uncomfortable for college students to talk about issues like sexual activity with the important adults in their lives.

However, there are a few questions that can help parents assess the situation or that might indicate potential problems or patterns of negative behavior with roommates that are frustrating their son or daughter.

- How's it going with your roommate?
- Does your roommate have a girlfriend/boyfriend? Is the friend in the room a lot? Does the friend ever spend the night?
- Do the other kids on the hall or the resident assistant know about this?

- How much sleep do you get at night?
- How were your grades on that first test/paper?
- Where are you finding it easiest to study—in your room or other places?

Parents can also choose to share stories about their own college experiences. Even if their teen scoffs at them, this can open the door to future family conversations.

Scenario 2: Two's Company; Three's a Crowd

Sarah wasn't sure what language her two roommates were speaking. She only knew she didn't understand a word they were saying and it was driving her crazy. Because they didn't bother to translate their comments, Sarah felt excluded by them. Whenever she came into the room to change clothes or pick up her textbooks, she felt like she was interrupting something. She was so uncomfortable in her new room that she tried to spend as little time there as possible.

When handling the situation by herself didn't seem to be working, Sarah finally turned to her mom for ideas. They had always been close and her mom was sympathetic, listening carefully to Sarah's tearful litany of complaints. Once Sarah had calmed down, her mother suggested that she schedule a meeting with the resident assistant to see if she could change rooms.

Sarah met with her RA to explain the problem, but was told she might have to wait a few months to change rooms. Upset and overwhelmed by the thought of having to stay in her current living situation one more day, she immediately began investigating college transfer.

By the next afternoon, Sarah had come up with a list of colleges to look into. However, over the weekend she was able to make some new friends on her dorm floor and began spending time in their rooms instead of her own. A few weeks later, Sarah was finally able to change rooms and she dropped the transfer idea entirely.

Parent Perspective

Sarah's mom had the right idea to encourage her daughter to approach her RA first about changing roommates. Colleges usually prefer that roommates try to work out their differences before taking the drastic step of changing rooms.

In further conversations, Sarah's mom also put some of the responsibility for Sarah's feelings of being mistreated back on her daughter by asking her if she had made any effort to make friends on her hall. Sarah was able to admit that she had been so stressed out about her relationship with the girls she'd been assigned to live with that she hadn't really attempted to connect with any other students in her dorm.

Pointing out to students who are in an unhappy living situation that there is a middle ground between leaving the university and suffering through the year with a miserable roommate situation can bring some balance to an emotionally laden situation like this one.

Her mom also suggested that Sarah try getting involved in either Ultimate Frisbee or intramural soccer, which she had enjoyed in high school. By the end of the week, Sarah called home to report that, though she still wanted to move out of the room, she was able to wait until her rooming situation could be worked out by residence life.

Parents should keep in mind that outgoing students like Sarah can usually make friends with people on their hall if they don't get along with their assigned roommate(s). This way they'll have someone to hang out with during the day, and will only need to be in their room to sleep until a new room assignment is made.

Another way parents can be supportive is to acknowledge and validate their child's feelings of disappointment that the new roommate(s) didn't work out as hoped or expected. Reinforcing the fact that this isn't the child's fault and that he or she will figure out ways to resolve this situation (that may or may not include college transfer) is helpful too. Regardless, all college students should have a stress-free space where they can relax, study, and sleep.

Roommate issues are common, but often the student is so upset that they can't think clearly about options they have. Questions, rather than statements, can often spark a useful dialogue about the situation.

- Have you tried to talk to your roommates about how it makes you feel when they don't include you in their conversations when you are right there in the room with them?

- Did you ask the RA if you, your roommates, and he or she could sit down together and work out a compromise until you get a new room assignment?
- Have you met any other students on your floor?
- Is there anyone else with a difficult roommate situation that you might be able to swap rooms with?
- Have you tried to get to know people in your classes or to join clubs where you can make new friends to spend time with?

Scenario 3: The Joke's on You

Adam, a freshman know-it-all, thought the housing questionnaire was ridiculous. He filled it out by giving the opposite responses to his real preferences for each question. To no one's surprise (except Adam's), his new roommate turned out to be an extremely poor match.

The roommate was an early riser who spent almost all of his time in the room playing Xbox games and listening to loud country music that Adam hated. When Adam invited friends to his room, his roommate put on his headphones and ignored everyone. The awkward atmosphere caused Adam to spend a lot of time in other people's rooms instead of his own.

One week, when Adam had been up late every night working on a project, his roommate woke him up before 7:00 a.m. three times in a row when he continued to hit the snooze button. The situation rapidly escalated to a shouting match and the RA, hearing the commotion, hurried down to calm the situation.

After this incident, Adam spent even more time away from his room. Realizing that he had created his own problems, he didn't attribute his difficult situation to the college itself. He soldiered silently through freshmen year and found a much more compatible roommate for his sophomore year.

Adam's roommate difficulties are different from the other stories in this chapter because he brought them on himself. Trying to outsmart the housing selection process, which is actually designed to help incoming freshmen be paired with a compatible roommate, is a bad idea with potentially unpleasant consequences!

Parent Perspective

Embarrassed when his snarkiness backfired, Adam never told his parents what he had done and kept his complaints about his living situation to a minimum. When they came for Parent's Weekend, Adam filled their time with sporting events, campus concerts, and restaurant dinners. His mom picked up on the fact that he and his roommate didn't seem to like each other or have much in common, but she wisely kept her thoughts to herself.

Luckily, Adam was mature enough to realize that the only problem with his new college was a direct result of his own actions. Given this, the situation was something he'd need to adapt to without involving either the college or his parents. Transfer was definitely not indicated in this example, nor was any parental input.

Scenario 4: We're Having a Party

Eliza didn't have a problem with her room; it was the whole building that bothered her. She didn't realize how much she craved quiet while studying until she moved into a freshman dorm in which the other students seemed to spend all their time partying.

At first, Eliza had lots of friends to do things with. However, as the weeks passed, her tendency to put studying first caused her to refuse a lot of social invitations. She saw less and less of her roommates as they were drawn into Greek life and the party scene. Though everyone was friendly to her during the day, once night arrived some of the girls began to actively exclude her and others just ignored her. No one in the dorm seemed to care about going to early morning classes or to be serious about turning assignments in on time.

Eliza complained to her parents and high school friends that her roommates didn't ever do their homework. Plus, they were always inviting other kids into the room to hang out when she was trying to get work done or sleep. The situation came to a head when the girls came in drunk, waking Eliza up at 3:00 a.m. the night before a big exam. Eliza tearfully told her parents that there had been a huge fight and now none of them were speaking to each other. The other girls on the hall took her roommates' side and thought she was a "loser."

Tired of the constant drama and feeling like there was no possible way to resolve the situation, Eliza begged to be allowed to transfer to a new school over winter break. Her parents encouraged her to request to be moved to a quieter dorm before taking this step.

Much to Eliza's surprise, the administrator in charge of housing was highly sympathetic and arranged for her to change rooms two weeks before finals. With a new living situation, her phone calls home soon became enthusiastic again and talk of changing colleges disappeared.

Parent Perspective

Eliza's parents had met her roommates when they dropped her off at her new college dorm that fall. The girls seemed friendly and outgoing and the RA made a point of introducing herself to them and sharing some of the dorm rules.

They had been relieved to hear that the dorm had quiet hours and that there was a policy that no overnight visitors were allowed during the week. The RA also reassured them that there was no drinking or smoking on her hall and that the school was very strict about disciplining students who didn't follow the rules.

Eliza's parents soon learned that none of this was true. They began receiving multiple texts and phone calls from Eliza. It seemed that all everyone did in her dorm was party and the RA was never around. "I'm pretty sure she's moved in with her boyfriend," Eliza confided.

Her parents were at their wit's end. They wanted Eliza to persevere and didn't really like the idea of having her start over again at a new school after only one semester. But they could also see that the dorm environment was taking a huge emotional toll on her. Her mother finally asked a friend who worked at a local university for some ideas. The friend suggested that Eliza ask the residential housing office if the college had substance-free or "quiet study" dorm options that she could relocate to.

If a student is not sleeping well or is having daily conflict with others, it can affect their entire outlook on college life. Parents may need to offer some practical solutions, even if they seem obvious.

- Can you use headphones when the noise is bothering you? Do you need better ones?

- Did you look into studying at the library or other quiet places on campus?
- Have you asked your roommates to try to be quiet after a certain hour on weeknights?
- What would you have to do to switch to a new room or dorm?

REASON TO TRANSFER: ACADEMICS

Ask any college freshman what the biggest difference is between high school and college and they will probably say "more freedom." Once in college, students are able to choose their own schedule, classes, major, and work habits. Increased college freedom also means increased student responsibility. The rhythm of each day becomes self-directed rather than teacher-directed.

Freshmen can be fooled by the amount of free time they think they have and fail to schedule sufficient time to complete the increased volume of reading and writing assignments expected in college. When students fall behind in classes, they may not feel comfortable reaching out for the academic support that is available, believing they should be able to manage on their own. Or they may blame the college for their stress and poor grades rather than their own study habits.

The pressure to choose a career path at the beginning of college is far greater than in the past. Some highly structured majors, like physical therapy, require academic commitment from the start. A percentage of students will decide on a definite career path in high school so their college choice is more straightforward. However, choosing a college based on a specific major can sometimes lead to problems. Many students need to try a variety of classes, and even majors, before settling on one. It is especially risky for a student with multiple career interests to attend a college with a narrow selection of majors.

Another group of teens try to satisfy their parents with an early career choice. This stifles the beat of their internal drummer. Finding a program that stimulates them may ultimately involve a college transfer as they mature and learn to make decisions on their own.

Scenario 1: All I Want Is My Fair Share!

Mona's parents viewed acceptance to one of the top U.S. colleges as the pinnacle of an illustrious high school career. To achieve this goal, they willingly paid for Mona's special summer camps, tutors, and college prep courses. They even sent their daughter overseas for a service learning experience in Central America during her junior year of high school.

The school guidance counselor assured them that, with Mona's grades and impressive slate of extracurricular activities, she was certain to be admitted to every college she applied to. Given this, when Mona wasn't accepted at her first choice school, she was disappointed. When she also didn't get into her second, third, or fourth selections, she was crushed. Then, unbelievably, she was wait-listed at her "safety" schools. Apparently Mona's profile wasn't what the various college admissions departments were looking for that year.

The family was horrified. Since her mother and father had followed a similar path to the one they'd set her on, they weren't sure what their next move should be. The guidance counselor suggested that Mona apply to a highly rated Canadian university. Shell-shocked, Mona and her parents agreed to give it a try. Anything would be preferable to a "B-list" American school.

Once there, a lack of adult support made it even more difficult for Mona to adjust to college life in a Canadian school she wasn't even sure she wanted to be in. In October she told her parents she was seriously considering transferring colleges. They immediately told her to reapply to all of the schools she'd previously been rejected from.

Mona flatly refused to do this. She had come to realize that having a real connection to other students and the faculty was more important to her than a college's prestigious reputation. She also decided she was tired of being around highly competitive students. She wanted to have the chance to apply the things she was learning to real-life situations instead of simply memorizing facts and following test-taking strategies.

When she tried to explain this to her mother and father, they dismissed her arguments and minimized how difficult the semester had been for her. After researching a number of American colleges, Mona came up with a short list of schools that seemed like they'd be a better fit for her. Without consulting her parents, she submitted transfer applications to them. When her acceptance letters arrived, she presented them to her parents, who grudgingly agreed to support her financially at whichever school she chose to transfer to.

Parent Perspective

Mona's parents were lukewarm about the college she ended up attending, something they expressed in obvious and subtle ways. They spent Parent's Weekend at the Canadian university comparing it unfavorably to the Ivy League colleges they had attended. When Mona had difficulty making long distance calls back to the States, they told her they'd figure it out over winter break. When she was worried that her advisor was pressing her to declare a major, they told her to "just pick something."

It's crucial that parents remember a few things when helping their teen choose a college where he or she will be both challenged and happy. First, it's important to remember that, no matter how much a student excels, there is absolutely no guarantee that this will entitle him or her to get into any college he or she applies to. Secondly, the school a student attends is no reflection on a parent's intelligence or parenting abilities. Finally, withdrawing financial or emotional support when a student's college experience doesn't turn out the way a parent wants it to will rarely be an effective strategy.

Unsurprisingly, acting in a critical or unhelpful manner often exacerbates an already tense situation. Asking the following questions might have resulted in a more open and useful dialogue with their daughter.

- What can we learn about the selective college admissions today (as opposed to a generation ago) that will help us understand the challenges and choices our daughter is facing?
- Could we all have a discussion of what an excellent college education means to each of us?
- How can we support our daughter in her university transfer?

Scenario 2: I Hate My Major!

Figuring out the velocity of an engine's turbine blades bored Paul. In fact, he disliked all his engineering classes. He felt like a misfit in them and it was disconcerting. After all, his grandfather and two uncles were engineers and they loved what they did. His parents were thrilled with his engineering major and often bragged to friends and relatives about what a great job he'd have when he graduated.

What Paul really looked forward to was his economics class. As the semester went on, he started thinking about a career in public policy and felt increasingly trapped. Although he wanted to get out of engineering and into another program, the type of public policy major he was really interested in wasn't offered at his technical university. He seriously considered transferring colleges but was afraid of his family's reaction.

Eventually he was helped by a cousin who described how he had been able to design his own major and get it approved when he was at college. This seemed like a good compromise to Paul. He ended up staying at his original university with a major in economics and a minor in engineering, mostly to keep the peace at home.

Sadly, this unusual combination didn't serve him very well. When he graduated, it took him much longer than many of his classmates to find a job, forcing him to live at home for almost a year while seeking employment.

Parent Perspective

Students often graduate with a different major than they initially started out with. Some students are able to change majors and remain at their original college. However, many more have experiences in which transfer ends up being the best option. Paul's and his parents' expectations about college majors were different and this continued to be the "elephant in the room" throughout his four years at college. If this situation sounds familiar, now might be a good time to take a personal inventory.

- Has your teen settled on a major yet? If not, can you live with them being undeclared or being enrolled in a more general liberal arts program?
- Does your son or daughter talk to you about his or her favorite classes and professors?
- Has your son or daughter ever asked you what career path you think he or she should choose?

- Have you unwittingly or blatantly expressed a preference for one major over another to your child, either directly or in conversations with someone else?
- Do you spend a lot of time talking about the monetary or social value of some professions over others?

Scenario 3: Decisions, Decisions

Madison knew within the first two weeks of class that she was definitely in the wrong major, and possibly the wrong college. She had dreamed of running her own interior design company someday but found the reality of her business classes at the urban university didn't match her ambitions at all.

When students presented projects together, Madison was always put in charge of the design aspects. She avoided discussions of the financial documents like the plague and thought the business majors were materialistic. With them, even discussions of fashion and apartments always came down to the cost of everything. She was interested in more creative endeavors, and she seemed to be on a different wavelength from most of her classmates.

The next semester Madison transferred to the Communications Department within the university. Her classes there were more engaging and she developed some close friendships. However, her grades were still on the low side and she found it difficult to get long-term projects completed. There was always an art opening or a concert that was more interesting than working on her presentations.

Finally, she decided to take some time off to figure out what to do next. After working in corporate customer relations for the summer, she decided to take a gap year traveling in Europe. Madison hoped that these two experiences would help her figure out whether transferring colleges would be the best choice for her.

Parent Perspective

Madison's parents were dubious when she broached the idea of changing her major. They saw business as a respectable profession with health care benefits, retirement plans, and a regular paycheck. They thought communications would be a hard field for her to find steady employment in.

Since Madison had always excelled at convincing others to see things her way, her parents agreed to let her give communications a try. When her grades didn't improve much over the next semester and she was unwilling to transfer back into the business department, they encouraged her to take a leave of absence and work in a communications-related field before deciding if a different college might meet her needs better. They also agreed to support her in a gap year if that was what she really wanted.

These days, there are no guarantees in the job market. Even historically stable fields like law and engineering can't always promise secure positions upon graduation. Before pushing a student in a certain career direction, it's important to consider the following questions.

- What is my child good at?
- What does my child spend a lot of time and energy doing?
- What do friends and relatives see as my teen's greatest strengths?
- What are the pros and cons of taking a gap year before deciding to transfer or remain at the same college?

Scenario 4: Freedom with Responsibility

"It's mine!" Jake yelled, chasing after the Frisbee flying across the college lawn. Compared to the nine- to ten-hour structured schedule he had been forced to follow in high school, his new college routine was a breeze. Jake only had classes for about four hours each day so he spent the rest of the afternoon hanging out with friends, working out at the gym, and checking Facebook at the college coffee shop.

Jake started his homework assignments after dinner just like he had in high school, but soon he found himself staying up later and later to complete them. There was much more reading for each class than he was used to and he had never been a strong reader. As he fell further and further behind in all his courses, he started to panic. He went to the college learning center and was assigned peer tutors for two of his classes. Because it was late in the semester, he still ended up with two Cs and two Ds.

When confronted by his parents, Jake vowed to work even harder. In the second semester, Jake was better organized, but once again he felt unprepared for the volume of homework and large research projects.

Although there was less assigned reading for his classes, there was more writing this time, which Jake struggled with as well.

During spring break he had a heart-to-heart talk with his parents in which he openly confessed that he wasn't sure he could handle college and was seriously considering dropping out. They expressed concern about his future and suggested he evaluate all his options first.

At the end of the semester, Jake met with his college advisor, who encouraged him not to give up. His advisor suggested that Jake consider transferring to a college that specialized in providing learning support. He told him about a friend's son who had successfully graduated from college after he addressed his learning issues by using a tutor along with software supports. The advisor recommended that Jake get an evaluation by a psychologist that specialized in educational testing in order to better understand what he needed help with.

Jake went home for the summer determined to find a college that would help him conquer his learning issues and stay in college until he graduated.

Parent Perspective

Jake's parents were thrilled when their son was accepted to three state schools. Because Jake had always had a tough time academically, despite all of their encouragement, they proudly told everyone they knew that he seemed to have "grown out of it" and was ready to start college with a fresh outlook. When Jake continued to receive poor grades, they were bewildered. How could he have been accepted to a good school and still not be able to keep up with the other students or complete his assignments in a timely fashion?

After reading an article in the *New York Times* about students with undiagnosed learning differences, Jake's parents realized that what was going on with their son wasn't unusual. There were actually colleges all over the country that had programs designed specifically for students who needed extra support with structuring their time and managing their course load. They immediately scheduled the evaluation Jake's advisor had suggested.

They also found quite a few resources on the National Center for Learning Disabilities site at www.ncld.org. This inspired them to contact an independent counselor specializing in Jake's type of learning differences in order to find the right educational programs for their son. Some of the questions they needed answers to included:

- Why is a psychological evaluation necessary in order to receive specialized learning support in college?
- What kinds of learning supports are available in college and how can my son/daughter access them?
- Where can I find a directory of independent college counselors who specialize in learning differences issues?

Scenario 5: Not a Theater Superstar!

Rachel discovered early on in her college experience that the required classes outside of her musical theater major were much easier than those at the selective arts academy where she had attended high school. She had chosen the college based on the excellent reputation of the theater program rather than the overall fit. Although she liked the program, the rest of the college experience seemed to be lacking for her.

On top of that Rachel realized that she didn't like living in a cold climate where it was often unpleasant to go running, her habit for stress relief. As the days went by, she found herself resenting the time that rehearsals were taking from all of her other interests.

Rachel had always had the lead in plays at her high school. She was very attractive and had a pleasing soprano voice. It was a shock to Rachel to discover that she was not considered one of the best actresses in the program. In fact, she was not even among the best freshmen. She found that she had to take extra voice lessons to improve her diction. In addition, her professors encouraged her to take additional dance classes to bring her technique up to par.

As the Spring Showcase neared, Rachel hoped that she would get a part in one of the short plays featured. Stress was evident in the halls and classrooms of the theater department. Rachel had made friends among her fellow actors in the fall, but now felt she was competing with a group of super "divas."

When the list of parts was posted, Rachel found that she did get a very small part as a maid, but it was not even a speaking part. Her parents had already booked a hotel room so that they could come and see the Showcase, but they wouldn't see much of her. After the Showcase, Rachel found that it was more fun to hang around the people from her dorm than to be among the intense theater crowd.

Gradually she began to realize that she'd rather pursue theater as an interest than a career. Rachel felt she was wasting her time and her parents' money at this particular college and the more she thought about it, the clearer it became that she would probably need to transfer. She left at the end of her freshman year, moving back home, where she could continue her studies part-time at both a local arts school and at a community college while she figured out her next step.

Rachel took the initiative to tour a number of different four-year colleges and universities during this time and really paid attention to both the academic and social opportunities that the schools offered. She also began to follow student comments on various blogs and websites to get an insider's view of each college.

After much consideration, she finally chose a liberal arts college that would allow her to pursue her interest in psychology while still being able to take part in college theater productions or nearby community theater.

Seventeen- and eighteen-year-olds like Rachel are learning and growing rapidly, right at the time they need to decide what college to attend. They often feel pressure to map out their entire career at this point in their life, even when the majority of them have no idea what they want to do. It's actually quite common to be undecided because whole disciplines and parts of life are unavailable for exploration in high school.

Students in talent-based majors like theater, music, and dance may find the competition unnerving, especially if they went to a small or rural high school. Suddenly they realize that their dreams of Broadway or Carnegie Hall may be somewhat unrealistic, despite what their mentors back home told them.

Additionally, many students often graduate with a different major than they initially enrolled with and research shows that the majority of college students will need preparation for multiple careers. Some students are able to change majors and remain at their original college. However, many more have experiences in which transfer ends up being the best option.

Parent Perspective

Rachel's mother and father were part of their community theater scene and both had aspired to be professional actors at one time. Rachel was their youngest child, the one with the talent. When they sent her to the private arts academy, they'd had high hopes that she would advance further in theater than they had.

When Rachel was accepted to a college where she would be able to study in a renowned musical theater program, her parents were ecstatic, feeling that she was well on her way to becoming a professional actor, the career they'd always envisioned for her. The evening that Rachel told them that she wanted to transfer, they were disappointed by what they perceived as her lack of commitment.

Thinking back on all the private lessons, summer arts camps, and auditions, they were tempted to put some parental pressure on her to try to stick it out "just a little longer."

However, they were able to keep their personal feelings about the transfer to themselves, while suggesting that Rachel try to combine theater with her new interest in psychology.

She agreed and took some theater classes before fully switching to a psychology major at her new college. Though both her mother and father struggled with feelings of loss, ultimately they realized that the choice was hers to make, not theirs.

After years of expensive lessons and camps, it is hard for parents to step back a bit in the college choice and let the student determine the career path to follow. Helpful questions to think about include:

- Is it possible for my son or daughter to have a dual major in the arts combined with something completely different?
- Is there a way that I can satisfy my love of theater, or music, or dance that doesn't depend on my child majoring in that discipline?
- When touring college campuses, have I allowed my child to explore different facilities and classes other than those dedicated to the arts?

REASON TO TRANSFER: FINANCES

Parents of freshmen can frequently be spotted on campus wearing t-shirts that read, "My child and all of my money go to [X] University." Though these shirts and bumper stickers may get a laugh, they're not as amusing in real life. Families should talk openly and realistically about what they can afford to pay for college and how this will impact the teen's choice of colleges. Some students are acutely attuned to the cost of college and how it affects their family, while others are quite oblivious.

Many factors figure into the cost of attending a college. Families need to understand that tuition, fees, and room and board are only part of the picture. Some financial aid awards expect students to earn a set amount of money during the summer to be used toward college costs. This means that money earned in a summer job can't go toward entertainment, as is often the case with a teen's high school job.

Transfers often choose to live off campus and be more independent. Housing is a significant part of the financial package and families should carefully add up the costs involved in apartment living. Unexpected costs may include Internet/cable charges, utilities (especially if the weather is extreme), parking, and even cleaning costs or repairs. A recent study by the Wisconsin HOPE Lab found that college net price calculators significantly over- or underestimated the cost of housing.

Parents should also be aware that not all colleges are up front about likely variations in financial aid packages over the four years. In addition, some majors may require a fifth or even sixth year to complete all of their requirements. Sometimes an unforeseen change in a family's finances such as a large medical bill or job loss can destroy even the best-laid family financial plan.

An inability to predict the future is one reason that it's so important for families to be cautious with student debt. Many teens are not used to dealing much with personal finances, even if they have a job, so it is important for them to learn skills like budgeting and responsible credit card use.

Scenario I: Money-Conscious Megan

Gaining admission to a highly selective university was quite an academic achievement for Megan. She was also relieved to earn several significant scholarships from the university. Her family did not have a lot of money, so she began college with the understanding that she'd need to supplement her scholarship aid with a well-paying summer job.

Megan's old high school position as a supermarket cashier didn't pay enough to meet her increased financial responsibilities. Once her last paper was handed in, she went out every day looking for employment. Unfortunately, Megan soon discovered that all the best positions had been filled by college students who had started their job search much earlier. Eventually she found a job waitressing in a restaurant. Though it paid more than cashiering, she still wasn't able to earn enough money to meet her college expenses for the coming year.

Once she returned to campus, Megan headed straight to the financial aid office of her college to seek help for the financial hole she felt like she was falling into. A friendly staff member helped her find a well-paying research job on campus. The added income made up her funding gap so she wouldn't have to transfer to a less expensive college.

Parent Perspective

Not all families have a feasible college budget to begin with. Family tensions can mount as high college tuition payments or unexpected expenses are added to regular household bills. This anxiety can double or triple when families have multiple children in college at once. Increased financial pressures can often result in a student needing to transfer to another college whether he or she wants to or not.

Mature students like Megan will show their independence and resourcefulness by finding ways to make ends meet. A student who is not as committed to a high-priced university as Megan was may find that the cost is not worth the strain on the family budget and decide to transfer.

Students may seem oblivious, but many are concerned about causing their parents any extra financial stress. Parents should talk openly and realistically with their teen right from the start about what they can and can't afford. Because financial circumstances can change rapidly, it's very risky for students and their families to choose a college that is outside of their financial means with the hope that the tuition payments will work out somehow.

It's important for parents to realize that treating students like the adults they're becoming can be an important part of the discussions. Students may even come up with some solutions that their parents hadn't even thought of. Talking points could include:

- Telling your child prior to college application season what you can reasonably afford for tuition payments each year
- Explaining the family budget and projecting the figures for the total cost of college attendance (including transportation, clothing, books, and extras) for at least four years
- Making sure your son/daughter knows what you expect them to contribute to the annual cost of their college

Scenario 2: Foreign Financial Fiasco

Fiona and her family were eagerly anticipating her opportunity to study abroad through her university's freshman program in Paris. However, as the departure date grew closer, Fiona grew apprehensive. Her language skills were not that impressive and she had never been away from home for longer than a weekend, let alone traveled by herself. Once she arrived in France, Fiona was placed with a host family that lived outside of the city. She felt quite isolated from her fellow freshmen.

As she began her classes, her inability to speak French fluently became more apparent and she found herself falling behind and becoming increasingly homesick. Fiona consoled herself by eating out a lot and shopping for clothes, shoes, and accessories. She ended up spending way too much money on things she didn't need. Her parents had given her a credit card before she left home so she began to use it for everything once she had gone through all her cash. Forgetting to keep track of the amount of money she was spending, Fiona's charges mounted steadily.

Her time in France wasn't at all what she had expected and Fiona couldn't wait for the semester to end so she could get back to her "real" life. Her relief at being home was short-lived, however, when her angry parents confronted her with the Visa bill. Embarrassed by what she had unwittingly done, Fiona tearfully told them that she would drop out of college and work full time until she repaid them.

This was not an acceptable solution to her parents. Fiona's next idea was to transfer to a local college and live at home, which would lower her parents' college expenses considerably. Her mother and father didn't like this solution either. They felt she should learn from her mistakes rather than run away from them.

Parent Perspective

Fiona's parents were shocked when they opened the credit card statement and saw the charges. Fiona had not had any type of job or work study while she was in Paris and there was no money left in her savings account. It was clear that she would be unable to pay any of the bill, with its exorbitantly high interest rates. This left the balance squarely in their court, along with Fiona's next tuition payment.

Her parents realized that having Fiona leave school and go to work was an extreme solution to the problem. Transferring colleges didn't seem like a good long-term solution either. Fiona's problems with budgeting and spending would follow her wherever she went to college unless she dealt with them.

They also understood that, given their daughter's cavalier attitude about money, giving her a credit card with a high limit to take to Europe had probably not been the wisest choice on their part. They admitted to Fiona that they should have sat down with her before she began college and discussed things like:

- Spending habits, budgeting, and balancing a checkbook/debit card each month
- Concepts like debt, overdraft, and service charges
- Credit card use and appropriate expenses (that is, medical emergencies or car repairs)
- Currency exchange and foreign exchange rates
- Ways to relieve stress that don't involve spending money

After much thought and honest discussion, Fiona returned to the university, got a part-time job in the school library, and created a repayment schedule in which she turned a portion of her checks over to her parents each month. As she began to whittle away at her debt, she realized just how much money she had wasted in France.

Determined not to ever have to deal with this situation again, Fiona purchased *Paying for College without Going Broke* by the Princeton Review staff, which provided some valuable tips on how to keep costs down during college.

REASON TO TRANSFER: REALITY CHECK

When families look at colleges, their primary focus tends to be on majors, courses, and professors' qualifications, along with things like campus safety and residence life. Many parents and teens just assume that the social parts of college life will just fall into place, which isn't always the case. Stories in this section highlight some of the discrepancies between what students thought college would be like and what they are actually dealing with once they arrive on campus.

These inconsistencies can evoke feelings ranging anywhere from mild culture shock, to acute misery, to depression. Each student's circumstances are different. Some will resolve situations themselves without requiring any adult intervention. Others may call for parental or administrative advice or action. Still others may require a college transfer.

Where a college is located geographically can be a huge factor in how a student adjusts to college life. Radically different parts of the country may be what teens look for in a vacation destination but may not be as desirable year round. Geographical regions can also affect the diversity of the student body, the types of foods available, recreational activities, and cultural opportunities, all of which are important to college students.

College athletes may face a different type of reality check. Students may discover that the level of competition is much steeper in college. They might not be able to make it to the first string, even if they feel they deserve to be there. Coaches who are bound and determined to have a winning season, no matter what it takes, can imply that it's easy to balance a rigorous practice schedule with the school's academic standards. In reality this can be grueling for a freshman athlete with a full course load.

Teens may also find that the campus culture isn't as accepting or supportive of their personality type or chosen lifestyle as their hometown or high school may have been. This can be both surprising and disillusioning to college students.

Scenario 1: Too Shy to Try

Michael had taken a personality/career assessment (Meyers Briggs Type Indicator) in high school. This designated him as an introvert. His parents were aware of this, as were his high school teachers. Michael himself was open about the fact that he frequently needed time by himself to recharge his energy. Despite this awareness, he failed to see any connection between his personality and the type of college he chose to transfer to.

Michael's first college was a small engineering school filled with students who had a similar lifestyle to his. After his freshman year he transferred to a large state university because he wanted to study creative writing instead of the computer engineering major he had originally been attracted to. Although the state university had planned several get-togethers at the beginning of the year for new transfer students, large social gatherings made Michael nervous so he didn't attend any of them.

In the past, he'd always preferred to hang out with one or two friends. Unfortunately, everyone at his new school seemed to already be in a group of friends. Michael dealt with his uncomfortable social situation by visiting Jeremy, his best friend from his old school, every other weekend. He spent the rest of his time alone in the off-campus apartment that he shared with a high school classmate, who was usually out with other friends.

This was too much "alone" time, even for Michael! He was just beginning to Google colleges closer to Jeremy's when an outgoing girl in his literature class invited him to join her book discussion group. As Michael became less self-conscious, he started going for coffee with a few group members after their meetings. Gradually his idea of transferring colleges again faded away. He even invited Jeremy to visit and meet his new friends.

Parent Perspective

Entering a new environment is highly stressful for someone who is naturally shy. This is intensified for the reticent transfer student who has to deal with all the uncertainties that come with meeting new people, taking new classes, and adjusting to a different campus in a relatively short time. Students with this type of personality often find it hard to acclimate as easily as transfers who are more socially confident.

Michael's parents were both extroverts, unlike their only son. Family communication tended to be brief and one-sided. Michael called his home once a week and the conversations focused on his grades and the quality of college food. Talking about how unhappy he was seemed like a taboo subject to Michael. Because he didn't tell his mother and father about his lonely and friendless situation and they never asked, his parents were unable to offer him the emotional support that might have made his college adjustment easier.

The family might have benefited from reading some of the books published on communicating with shy or quiet college students, such as:

- *You're on Your Own* by Marjorie Savage
- *The Happiest Kid on Campus* by Harlan Cohen
- *Quiet: The Power of Introverts in a World that Can't Stop Talking* by Susan Cain

Their son's first transfer was very appropriate for academic and career reasons, even though the size of the school stretched his comfort level. Changing colleges a second time, before the semester was even over, would probably not have been advisable in this case.

Parents of introverted teens need to consider whether having a challenging time socially is a valid reason for their son or daughter to transfer. Michael would continue to be shy and still have trouble making friends no matter where he went to college. The following questions will help parents familiarize themselves with their son or daughter's social life and level of engagement so that they can understand why transfer may be an attractive option.

- Have you been in touch with your friends from your first college?

- When we come to visit can we take you and a few friends out for dinner?
- What do you have planned for this weekend?
- Have you joined any clubs? Are there any campus activities that appeal to you?

Scenario 2: On the Outside Looking In

Many of Katelyn's high school friends were interested in New England colleges, but she loved her tour of the big southern university with the magnolias in bloom and the Admissions Office staff's southern hospitality. Katelyn was also ecstatic about the prospect of joining a sorority, playing tennis through the winter, and being immersed in the campus social life. She could already picture herself dressing up in the school colors and going to the football games with some of the friendly students she met on her campus visit.

Though her parents were concerned about the distance from their Vermont home, Katelyn convinced them that she would feel right at home in the South. When she arrived on campus, she quickly made friends with her roommate and the girls on her hall. Shortly afterward, she became involved in a whirlwind of Greek rush activities and parties. There were several sororities that she liked and Katelyn, who had been popular in high school, felt sure she would get a bid from all of them.

The whole campus was caught up in the excitement of rush week. On bid day, Katelyn woke up earlier than usual. She couldn't wait to find out who her new sorority sisters would be! She was shocked and miserable when she didn't receive a single bid. Katelyn remembered some of the sorority girls mimicking her accent a few weeks ago. She had assumed that they were joking but perhaps they hadn't been.

Her confidence was so badly shaken by the whole experience that, after talking to her family, she decided to transfer to a large northern university, where she was accepted into her mother's college sorority.

Parent Perspective

Katelyn's parents were concerned about her attending the southern university primarily because of the distance from their home. The North/South dynamic wasn't even on their radar. There had been no prior indicators, either in the admissions materials or on the campus visit, that Katelyn's northern background would be an issue once she arrived on campus. The overall feel of a campus can be much different on a tour that has been orchestrated by the college than the day-to-day reality of the place.

Some colleges actively recruit students from other regions to diversify their student bodies. Therefore it isn't in their best interests to be open about any difficulties students from other parts of the country may encounter once enrolled. Despite what college administrators may think, the dominant student culture does matter because it affects things like Greek life, clubs, and student organizations.

All colleges have a distinct ecology (or environment) that is determined largely by the student body, although the core values of the college and the composition of the faculty also play a role in it. When the school's culture doesn't match the student's expectations, they will feel isolated and uncomfortable. Students are far less likely to transfer from a college where they find a niche that includes friends and activities they enjoy.

A few steps that Katelyn and her parents could have taken to assess the college culture at the school and in the surrounding community include:

- Spending time eating at local restaurants, reading the hometown newspaper, and talking with residents to get a feel for the area
- Requesting that Katelyn be allowed to sit in on a few classes or spend an overnight at the university before committing to the school
- Speaking with an independent college consultant to get his or her input on the college's social culture
- Visiting a site like College Confidential to see what other students had to say about the social atmosphere of the college

Scenario 3: Culture Counts

Olivia grew up in Oregon but always dreamed of going to college for environmental engineering. She was an avid reader of the *U.S. News & World Report* guide to colleges, so she decided it would be an exciting adventure to attend college on the East Coast. She began her freshman year at a university in New York State.

Her new school had a phenomenal engineering program. Olivia was so stimulated by her classes and professors that she didn't even mind the increased homework. However, she found the small town the college was located in boring. There were only a few bars and fast food restaurants, a bowling alley, and a rundown movie theater on the main thoroughfare. Olivia was used to a lively arts and music scene with plenty of ethnic restaurants. Now, instead of sushi, independent films, and classical concerts, her weekend choices were narrowed down to off-campus parties, eating junk food, or hiking the many nearby trails in the area.

Olivia also discovered that the other students didn't share her enthusiasm for engineering or the arts. Without any good friends to talk about things she was passionate about, she felt increasingly cut off from the "real" world.

Winter came early, with gray skies and snow nearly every day. As the semester dragged on, Olivia's social life wasn't improving. Feeling lonely and isolated, she found herself calling home more frequently than she wanted to. With the college so far away, her parents also contacted her on a regular basis to make sure she wasn't becoming depressed.

Over winter break, Olivia's parents broached the subject of her transferring to an engineering school in a more urban environment. Olivia thought this was a great idea. She began looking at other colleges online and found three city universities that were closer to Oregon that offered courses very similar to those she loved in her current school. With a plan in place she and her parents felt much better.

Shortly after Olivia submitted all of her transfer applications for the fall, she began to date another engineer. He shared many of her interests and had a car. Secure in her new relationship, Olivia decided that her current college wasn't so bad after all. Though she had been accepted at two of the three schools she applied to transfer to, she told her parents that she had changed her mind and would stay where she was until she graduated.

Parent Perspective

With Olivia at a school that was several thousand miles away, her parents weren't sure how they could best help her when it was obvious she was struggling. Their initial plan was to try to support her through her freshman year at the New York school, then work with her to assess what her next step should be. Together, they came up with a list of ways that they could encourage her to improve her situation there:

- Send her the latest novels and DVDs
- Mail her regular care packages with some treats from her favorite candy store
- Suggest that she try some of the outdoor activities other students seem to enjoy like hiking, ice skating, or cross-country skiing
- Encourage her to talk to her advisor or a counselor about what other kids who feel lonely have done to try to improve their situation, such as joining clubs or studying abroad

Not only did her parents support Olivia's decision to transfer, they also helped her research schools and finalize her essays. When she decided to stay in New York, they were initially upset, feeling she had wasted their time and money. They urged her to at least visit a few of the colleges she had been accepted to so they could all feel confident that she was making the right decision. Olivia politely refused.

Concerned that she was making an important decision based on a new relationship, her parents were frustrated. They made it clear that they would not bail her out again, either financially or by helping her facilitate a quick transfer, if her decision to stay didn't end up working out the way she wanted it to.

Olivia's parents had a tough freshman year too! However, instead of forcing the situation, they were able to remain supportive while making their expectations clear and setting some boundaries around what they would and wouldn't do in the future. As hard as this can be to do, sometimes it's the best course of action, especially when distance is a factor.

Scenario 4: College Athletics

Courtney had been playing hockey year round since she was four and had always assumed that she would be recruited by one of the top Division I hockey programs. Although her skills were excellent, she was slightly slower than some of the other top players. She was only recruited by Division III schools where coaches indicated she would get a lot of playing time.

Although Courtney liked the supportive learning environment at some of the liberal arts Division III schools she visited, she still chose to go to a Division I hockey power as a walk-on athlete rather than a recruited one.

The Division I coach was inspirational and pushed Courtney to raise the level of her conditioning and her game, but she still found herself sitting on the bench week after week. The hockey situation was stressful enough, but Courtney was also struggling in classes like history and English that required a lot of reading and memorization and her other grades had dropped as well. At the end of freshman year, she decided that she needed to sort out her priorities and find a Division III college that was a better academic match to transfer to.

Parent Perspective

Surprisingly, the impact that high school athletics can have on college success is huge. Some student athletes have been dreaming about playing their sport in college (or even the pros) since they were in elementary school. It's extremely difficult for them to comprehend the odds they are up against. Understanding that there are approximately twenty-two thousand high schools but only about four thousand American colleges gives families a better sense of just how competitive college sports are.

Multiple factors figure into college sports recruiting, including the competitiveness of the student's high school, early coaching, having the opportunity to play in national tournaments, and the devotion and commitment of the student's family to the sports scene. Competition for the starting spots on the team is intense.

Students are often surprised and disappointed to discover that they may have limited opportunities once they arrive at their new college. Star high school athletes may seethe with frustration when they are forced to sit on the bench in college. They may even consider transferring colleges in order to get more playing time.

How can mothers and fathers best help their teen assess the validity of wanting to transfer colleges because of a sports-related issue?

- Use their knowledge of how much structured, physical activity their son or daughter needs to keep a positive attitude and maintain good health and study habits

- Work with their teen to assess the social and academic fit of the college if the sport were suddenly taken out of the equation
- Encourage their son or daughter to explore the possibility of getting involved in intramural or club sports if the school's varsity sports program isn't meeting his or her needs
- Obtain a second opinion about the student's talent and long-term future in the sport from the coach of a club team or summer camp

A final thing to be aware of is that injury can strike student athletes at any time, making competition in sports impossible. When this happens, a poor college match will quickly become even more evident and transfer may be the best choice for the student. A few other questions that could be pertinent include:

- Would the athlete still choose the college he or she is transferring to if he or she couldn't play the sport?
- What is the likelihood of financial support for the transfer athlete at the school?
- Has the student met the other members of the team?
- If the athlete's major becomes too demanding, could the athlete play at the club or intramural level?

Scenario 5: Athletics and Academia

Tasha was a strong athlete and a good student during high school. She was heavily recruited by several colleges for her grades and basketball skills. Because her family didn't have any extra money for college, she decided to begin her freshman year at a prestigious university that had offered one of the best financial packages. She initially enrolled as premed, but soon realized that it was going to be next to impossible to maintain the grade point average that she needed to keep her financial aid while continuing to play Division I basketball.

The travel schedule for varsity basketball was brutal. Unlike her teammates, Tasha had a hard time sleeping on the bus, which meant she was exhausted when she returned from away games. Her level of fatigue made it hard to concentrate on homework, even when she disciplined herself to go to the library.

Though she went to all the review sessions for her classes and made full use of tutoring and advising offered by the academic advisor assigned to the team, she was still finding it hard to keep up. In addition to this, Tasha felt like her college life was dictated by sports and homework. She had no time for a social life or to explore campus activities. She felt like she was missing out on the full college experience.

After much soul-searching, Tasha decided that the financial and emotional cost of the pre-med program, combined with basketball, was just too much. Having financial security and minimal loans to pay off after graduation was as important to her as having a challenging career in health care. She talked with her team's advisor about her concerns. Together they came up with a plan for her to transfer to one of the smaller public colleges that had initially recruited her for basketball, where she could change her major to radiology, still play her sport, and afford the tuition.

Some students, especially those who receive athletic scholarships and for whom academic success comes easily, will need to be careful about balancing the athletic requirements of their scholarships with keeping their grades up. Many students believe that they can continue to balance academics and sports in college as they did in high school. However, college academics and activities can be far more intense.

Parent Perspective

Stepping back isn't the same as being uninvolved or disinterested. Parents don't always need to take a lead role in their son or daughter's educational process. College is a time when students begin to make their own decisions for their future. Tasha's parents had both attended community college part-time and Tasha was the first of their children to attend a four-year college. They had little experience with the demands of high-level athletics and academics.

They were extremely proud of their daughter's hard work and strong organizational skills during high school, which had resulted in her generous scholarship. To them it seemed like the most helpful thing they could do was to support her in whatever decisions she made. Whenever they started to feel anxious about her leaving the prestigious university, they reminded themselves of all of the ways Tasha showed her responsible nature, including:

- Earning money to offset her living costs during school breaks and summer vacations
- Taking charge of her college and transfer applications
- Communicating often with her family to let them know what was going on in her life

Their attitude of "she's responsible, it's her future" acknowledged Tasha's maturity and long-term goal of having a career she was interested in without a huge debt load.

Scenario 6: Noninclusive Campus

Zach spent a lot of time during his junior year in high school visiting colleges, studying for SATs so he would get high scores, and thinking about what he'd like to major in so he'd be sure to choose the university that would be the perfect fit for his career goals. When he was accepted at a renowned research university, both he and his family were delighted. Stepping onto the spacious, historic campus, Zach was sure he had made the right decision.

A month into his freshman English class, several male students began to make snide remarks under their breath about Zach's sexual orientation. Though he ignored them, the whispered comments escalated and soon afterward Zach began to find derogatory notes taped to the door of his dorm room. When he received an obscene message via text, Zach began to worry that he might be physically harmed by his tormentors. He resolved to report the incidents to the Dean of Students.

Much to his surprise, the dean minimized the harassment, saying, "It sounds like a student prank. If you're worried, you can go to the Health Center." Nonplussed, Zach responded that he wasn't sick, which was met with an indifferent shrug. "Just tough it out then," suggested the dean.

The next time Zach was singled out in the school dining hall, he scheduled a meeting with the provost, which was even more dismaying. "You might be bringing this on yourself by the way you dress. Try to tone it down and see what happens," was the college administrator's advice. Zach attempted to push back and explain that he felt he was being discriminated against. The provost retorted, "Maybe this isn't the right environment for you." Stunned and mortified by the whole encounter, Zach returned to his room to find a sexually explicit drawing had been pushed under his door.

After tossing and turning most of the night, he decided to transfer to a college with Lesbian, Gay, Bisexual, Transgender, Queer (LGBTQ) services and an active gay community. Browsing through college sites, he was able to identify several schools that seemed like a good fit. Though they weren't as renowned for the type of scientific research that he was most interested in, they all had strong academic programs and seemed to offer a social atmosphere that would be more accepting than what he'd found at his current university.

Zach finished the semester with excellent grades. Then, with the support of his parents, he arranged to transfer to a smaller liberal arts college after winter break.

Parent Perspective

Zach had come out as a gay male in ninth grade. He attended a liberal high school with an active LGBTQ student group in a diverse community. Neither he nor his parents had even considered that the social atmosphere might be different in college. They were all so used to others accepting his sexual orientation that it was a nonissue for them when looking at colleges. Some questions the family could have asked on their college visits include:

- How tolerant is the campus to different groups (racial, religious, and sexual)?
- Are there active LGBTQ organizations on campus?
- Are town residents accepting of diversity in the college's student population and faculty members?
- How does an LGBTQ organization like Campus Pride (https://www.campusprideindex.org/) rate the college or university?

For LGBTQ students, discovering that there are no policies in place or laws to protect them from harm or harassment in college can be devastating. Not only that, but dealing with insensitive, unsupportive, or indifferent administrators may come as a shock. Students may find it difficult to concentrate and focus on their academic studies if they constantly feel threatened or unsafe.

Failure to find like-minded students and faculty on campus to connect with can be depressing and isolating for LGBTQ teens. Parents can remind their son or daughter that not everyone feels the way they do and that the academic reputation of a university needs to be balanced with its social climate.

Another important way parents can assist their son or daughter in this type of situation is to help them evaluate whether the harassment is an isolated incident or institutional prejudice. This will likely be a major consideration in whether the teen decides to transfer or not.

2

LESS COMMON TRANSFER SCENARIOS

OVERVIEW

Every transfer has a story to tell. Sometimes the reasons for the transfer are not easy to discuss, particularly where substance abuse, mental health, or immaturity are involved. When a student has a college experience that doesn't work out as planned, his or her parents' anxiety and desire to micromanage the transfer process may increase. There are no guarantees of a good transfer, but there are certain action steps (discussed by experts, parents, and students later in this guide) that can make successful transfer more likely.

REASON TO TRANSFER: COPING WITH CRISIS

Going to college is a natural progression, a rite of passage for many teens. Some students may arrive on campus with a preexisting medical or psychiatric condition; others can develop a medical issue while in college. Students should be encouraged to take as much responsibility for controlling their medical condition as soon as possible because it will likely be a part of their life from now on.

This doesn't mean that parents should disengage completely from the student, especially if they want their son or daughter to succeed in college. This is particularly true of a teen that transfers colleges following the onset of a medical difficulty. Not only will he or she be coping with a new lifestyle related to his or her recent diagnosis, but he or she will most likely be dealing with feelings of loss (the dream of how college was supposed to go), confusion, shame, and disappointment while trying to adjust to a new environment.

Sometimes parents may suspect, based on high school experiences, that their teen could be more susceptible to drug and alcohol abuse or self-destructive behaviors like eating disorders than the average college freshman. But just as frequently it can be hard for adults to differentiate between what is normal teen experimentation and what qualifies as an addiction or serious problem.

Deciding when to intervene becomes twice as difficult when the teen enters a new, less-structured environment in a town where he or she is just another anonymous college student and adult monitoring is minimal to nonexistent. Added to this, at many colleges continuous heavy partying or eating disorders are often viewed as a badge of honor and a chosen lifestyle rather than as serious medical issues.

Some teens will be diagnosed with a mental illness such as depression during their time in college. This won't necessarily prevent them from continuing to be enrolled in college, but may entail some extra support from college personnel, the surrounding community, and their family. Students who have worked through intense issues such as substance abuse, eating disorders, or psychiatric problems, then transferred to a new school, often feel removed from their peers, who haven't experienced the challenges they have.

Eighteen- and nineteen-year-olds are not generally anxious about their health. Cancer and other serious medical issues come as a real shock to them. Students facing major health challenges (short or long term) may find they'll need to transfer closer to home, where they can get family and medical support.

Other crises that can greatly impact young people are college-related crises like another student's sudden death by suicide, a drug overdose, or a car accident. Issues around a student's sexuality or an academic crisis like probation or getting expelled can also influence a student's desire to transfer colleges.

Scenario 1: Alcoholism

Trevor had been expelled from his first college because of a serious drinking problem that led to problems in his dorm and an escalating conflict with a professor. After months of chaos, confusion, and midnight phone calls, he agreed to enter a therapeutic program to deal with his alcoholism.

A year later, Trevor's therapists and parents agreed that he was ready to go back to college. This time, Trevor selected a private liberal arts college closer to home. His parents were pleased, feeling that the close-knit community would be more supportive of their son during his recovery.

His first day back at college, Trevor was miserable. He found the orientation events at the college babyish. He didn't want to play the icebreaker games or participate in the dorm scavenger hunt. The next day, he skipped out on most of the scheduled activities, so he didn't meet many other transfer students.

Things got better once classes started up, but Trevor still wasn't totally comfortable at his new college. Most of the weekend activities revolved around dressing in blue and gold, going to the football games (with a flask of alcohol), and celebrating afterward with late night parties. Trevor knew that he couldn't afford to go down that addictive road again.

Though he had a single room, he felt like the students on his substance-free hall were too judgmental. He couldn't seem to find any friends who shared his interests. Trevor spent most of his free time in his room listening to music and texting friends from his rehabilitation program.

Over winter break, he told his parents that he couldn't stay at the school any longer. His parents, his therapist, and his sponsor disagreed. They encouraged him to get involved in the campus branch of Alcoholics Anonymous (AA) and find a local sponsor as well, preferably someone in their late twenties, who would understand some of the age-related issues he was struggling with. They explained to Trevor that changing colleges again wouldn't solve his relationship problems. They would do anything they could to support him, but he had to do most of the work himself instead of running away.

Grudgingly, Trevor agreed to give their suggestions a try. Much to his surprise, when he attended his first campus AA meeting, he saw students there who he had always felt were college superstars. Slowly he began talk about his fears and concerns with the group. Though he had a few minor relapses with alcohol, it seemed like his new sponsor and some of the other students really understood what he was going through and how he felt. As Trevor's alcohol-free social life improved, so did his grades and his attitude.

Parent Perspective

Parents with students like Trevor will need to make sure that their child has the proper support at college, as well as keeping the lines of communication between all of them intact. Mothers and fathers must carefully balance the need for adult involvement with their student's age-appropriate desire for independence. Some steps concerned parents can take include:

- Encouraging their son or daughter to join a support group on campus such as Alcoholics Anonymous, Narcotics Anonymous, or Overeaters Anonymous
- Setting up a regular time to speak in person weekly, either by visiting, via the phone, or on Skype; reminding the student that they can call home any time, day or night
- Arranging for a trusted adult (other than the parents) to occasionally check in with the student. This person could be a therapist, a member of the clergy, or a family friend
- Exploring additional resources with their son or daughter such as the Association of Recovery in Higher Education (http://collegia terecovery.org/faq/)

Scenario 2: Severe Anxiety

Anxiety attacks are often minimized by those who don't understand how debilitating they can be. Symptoms can include trouble breathing, a pounding heart, or even passing out. Most people become anxious in an unfamiliar situation, but for some students, the physical and emotional reactions surpass normal bounds and can be incapacitating.

Joe had his first serious attack during the PSATs. He had to leave the room to calm down and wasn't able to finish the test. A second attack occurred, with the same outcome, while Joe was taking the SAT as a junior. With this history, it felt like a huge victory to him when he not only completed the SAT in the fall of his senior year, but scored highly on it. Because he got good grades in his advanced classes at his high school and never had the attacks anywhere else, Joe and his parents were convinced they were related to the stress of taking standardized tests.

When Joe applied to college, at his parent's urging he included several highly rated colleges on his list. When the final decision time arrived, Joe was torn between the allure of a well-known urban university and a smaller, less prestigious college that he felt drawn to. The university was strong in pre-law, an interest of Joe's, and the family was offered a generous financial aid package. Ultimately, the challenge of the larger university, coupled with his parents' pride and excitement about his acceptance there, won out.

From the beginning Joe felt intimidated by the size of the university. Everything from class registration to using the library seemed unfamiliar and complicated. Each day he had to stand in a long line for something, from obtaining a student ID to getting a bus pass. Joe found it difficult to find a quiet place to collect his thoughts during the day. Although he felt overwhelmed, he was too nervous and self-conscious to approach anyone at the university to get some support. He began to question whether he had made the right college choice.

One afternoon he found himself unable to breathe properly. He was able to calm himself by breathing into a paper bag. Two days later he had another anxiety attack and was forced to seek help at the university clinic. At this point, Joe finally admitted to his parents that he was struggling at school.

Parent Perspective

Joe's parents knew about the anxiety attacks he'd had in high school, but they dismissed them as being brought on by the pressures of standardized testing. Fortunately, when Joe started having these attacks again during his freshman year, his parents took it seriously. They felt guilty for weighing in so heavily on the side of the prestigious urban university when Joe was making his choice. Additionally, they blamed themselves for not realizing that, given his temperament, a large competitive college might be a less than optimal atmosphere for him.

Once they heard he was having a hard time adjusting to the college, Joe's mother and father drove up to campus to spend time with him on the weekends. They helped him get oriented to his new city by taking long walks together and checking out the different eating options that Joe could take advantage of with his flex dining dollars.

As the semester progressed, Joe's parents made sure they were available to talk with him daily and they sent regular care packages. They also encouraged him to join a debate club and to invite some of his new friends home for the weekend. Additional ideas for parents in support of an anxious student include:

- Sharing contact information with the student's roommate(s) in case the student retreats from everything due to anxiety
- Helping the student establish a mentor relationship with an RA, faculty member, or family friend early in the semester so that the student has someone to turn to when anxiety hits
- Talking with the student about a reasonable course load and the problems of taking on too much

Scenario 3: Health Issues—Temporary and Chronic

Suzanne was very happy at the small conservatory she had chosen. The students were diverse and a little bit quirky, just her style. She took full advantage of college her first semester, packing her schedule with a variety of interesting classes, volleyball, and membership in a choral group. By the second semester, she began to feel tired all the time and was barely able to drag herself to class, let alone practice for the choral concert. One day she fainted in volleyball and was taken to the health clinic on campus. She took it easy for the next few days while she waited for the lab results.

Shaken by her diagnosis of leukemia, she immediately returned home to confer with her family. Suzanne missed two weeks of classes but was able to make up her work and complete all of her courses. Her treatments over the summer exhausted and depleted her, even though her mother helped in every possible way. In the fall, Suzanne made the difficult decision to transfer to a local liberal arts college where she could take a reduced load of classes, receive treatment from her local hematologist, and live at home.

Mariah loved her newfound independence in college. She and her roommate Shelby tried out many different clubs and activities. Her classes were stimulating and she was doing well in them until she lost her appetite and found it difficult to get out of bed for class. Her roommate became concerned as the days dragged on and there was no improvement. Mariah was reluctant to call her parents even after she went to the clinic and was diagnosed with mononucleosis. She thought she would get over it on her own and decided not to worry her parents.

Because Mariah had not waived her rights to her academic and health records stemming from the FERPA law, the university never contacted her parents. Finally, Shelby called her roommate's mom and she came right away. Mariah spent several months at home recovering her strength. Eventually she was able to return to campus and make up her incomplete coursework the next semester.

Parent Perspective

In Suzanne's case, transfer was the only option because of the severity of her diagnosis and the intense nature of the treatment she would require. Realistically Suzanne probably wouldn't have been able to maintain her course load while trying to manage her illness. Additionally, college dorm life isn't really compatible with serious illness. The strain on the family finances that would result from commuting back and forth every week was the final factor in the family's decision to have her transfer closer to home.

Though she loved the conservatory and was devastated to have to move to a local four-year school, she and her parents agreed that the health department at her first college wasn't equipped to offer the level of physical and emotional support that she'd require. In a case like this, parents need to initiate and support the student's decision to transfer as well as to be supportive and understanding of the multiple losses this results in for their son or daughter.

Mariah's situation was far less serious than Suzanne's. Nevertheless, a dorm is usually a poor place to recover from any illness that drags on. Parents should talk to their son or daughter about how to approach health problems before he or she leaves for college. They should also have their college student sign a FERPA waiver so that they are informed if serious health issues arise. Parents who are concerned about their child's health during college should consider the following additional steps:

- Share contact information with the student's roommate in case problems arise
- Evaluate the distance to hospital facilities and their quality if your son or daughter has a chronic condition such as asthma
- Check on the procedure for obtaining prescriptions on campus

Scenario 4: Eating Disorder

When Katherine met Ashley once every few weeks for breakfast, she didn't notice that Ashley only ate a small helping of fruit or a few bites of low-fat yogurt. Katherine realized that Ashley was very thin, but there were lots of thin girls in college, so she didn't think much about it.

One day, as they were walking to class after breakfast, Ashley turned pale and suddenly had to sit down. Concerned, Katherine walked her over to the nearby health clinic. It was a shock when Katherine heard later in the day that Ashley had needed to leave college after being diagnosed with a number of serious physical ailments related to her anorexia. Ashley returned home to Alabama to be taken care of by her family and her doctor.

Unbeknownst to her friend, Ashley had spent a lot of time coping with anorexia in high school. Eventually, with the help of family members and a counselor specializing in eating disorders, she had gotten to the point where she was able to maintain a healthy weight and eating habits. Considering herself cured, she entered a prestigious university over one thousand miles away from her hometown.

It was hard to return home to face the same problems and Ashley struggled in a treatment program for several months. Slowly, with counseling and proper diet, she regained her health. As she became ready to return to college, her family urged her to consider transferring closer to home.

Over several months, Ashley visited a few colleges and universities in Alabama, but they just didn't feel right. She had loved the academic challenge and the beautiful New England setting of her prior university. Her parents relented and she reentered her school in the fall with a few stipulations. At times it was quite a struggle for her to avoid her old dietary habits, particularly when things weren't going well with her classes. However, she persevered and was able to graduate on time with her class.

Parent Perspective

Given her medical history, Ashley's parents were nervous about how their daughter would deal with the stress of a rigorous academic environment so far from home. While she was recovering, her mother and father really pushed the idea of her transferring to a college closer to them, but Ashley insisted that she wanted to return to her school. After much negotiation, her parents agreed to allow her to reenter the university providing that she checked in regularly with her nutrition counselor and therapist.

Ashley's medical diagnosis would have been a legitimate reason for her to transfer to a less stressful college atmosphere. A crucial piece of the equation was that she didn't want to leave her first university. Because giving Ashley more control over her own life was an important part of her treatment for anorexia, her parents agreed to give the college a second try with some nonnegotiable parameters in place.

Parents should be also aware that eating disorders are becoming increasingly common for young men. Traditionally, eating disorders show up most often among dancers and gymnasts. However, sports like wrestling and lightweight crew can also make unhealthy eating habits more likely due to the pressure to "make" a certain weight. Parents should:

- Work out a mutually agreeable plan for regular counseling and nutritional coaching
- Schedule home visits during breaks so that they can evaluate how the student is adapting to the planned counseling

REASON TO TRANSFER: RESTLESSNESS

The beginning of freshman year is full of excitement, like an electrical force. New friends, new academic subjects, and a new living environment all energize college freshmen. As the novelty wears off, some students enter a restless period. They feel like a certain spark is missing from their college experience. This may push them to initiate transfer in the hopes of restoring the incredible energy they felt at the beginning of college. It's important to note that this restlessness is not necessarily due to a poor college match.

Searching out new subjects and situations is a natural part of college life. However, this exploration should not always be taken to the extreme of transferring colleges. College should also encourage students to eventually develop some in-depth focus in an area of study. This won't happen if the student flits from college to college.

Scenario 1: No Moss Grows on Ariel

Ariel loved drama and adventure. Sudden changes in plans and completing her school projects at the very last minute didn't fluster her at all. She thrived on constant change. Changing groups of friends, boyfriends, and hair styles and color on a regular basis didn't faze her in the least.

Ariel began her college career at a small college about an hour from home. Initially she relished the freedom of choosing her classes and deciding how she wanted to spend her free time. By March, the novelty of being away from home had worn off and the small college seemed a bit too confining to Ariel. She decided to transfer to a large public college that fall. Initially she found the buzz of activity on campus at all times of the day and night exciting. But after one semester she was bored with the friends she'd made and didn't like her large lecture classes in psychology and English.

Her parents thought she should give the university more of a chance. Ariel disagreed. In search of the perfect college experience, she transferred to a medium-sized private university. Her latest school had smaller, more personal classes than the second college and more academic choices than her first college. Still, there were elements of both her prior college experiences that she missed. She remembered how she had loved going to the basketball games at the large college and she missed some of her freshman friends from the first college.

As Ariel was starting to discover, transferring frequently can get in the way of deeper learning and forming strong social connections. Truly belonging to a college community sometimes takes time and Ariel had yet to give any one college more than a year.

Parent Perspective

The first time Ariel initiated transfer, her parents decided that maybe a larger school was better for her in the long run, so they didn't argue with her. They drove to visit her in good spirits, anticipating a relaxed visit with their youngest daughter. Much to their dismay, over dinner Ariel informed them that she still hadn't really found what she was looking for in a college, so she had begun researching several other schools to transfer to for the spring semester. Her horrified parents begged her to at least finish out the year at her current school, but she was adamant that it "just wasn't right for her."

Unsure how to intervene in her runaway train approach to higher education, her baffled parents stayed quiet. However, their apprehensions and feelings that maybe they should be doing something to put the brakes on this less than ideal situation grew daily.

Eventually they decided they needed to speak with someone in the college world who had been through this type of situation before and could offer them some input and suggestions. They were able to get an appointment with a college counselor, who recommended that they encourage Ariel to:

- Work closely with a career counselor at her school to help her find a major that she was really interested in
- Pay for any transfer-related costs out of her own savings
- Find volunteer work, take on a job, or apply for an internship at college

Scenario 2: When the Honeymoon Is Over

Initially, Brandon was very happy with his acceptance at a mid-sized college in Wisconsin. He liked the positive atmosphere in his classes and felt comfortable hanging out with kids who were from similar backgrounds.

After a few semesters, he began to realize that the predictability of the students often made him feel like he knew what they were going to say before they said it. Brandon enjoyed passionate debates about things like politics and gun control, but he found that most of the students stuck together on one side of the question or the other. He was also having trouble deciding on a major and couldn't seem to find any choices that really interested him.

By the spring of his sophomore year, Brandon began to feel like he needed to be somewhere, anywhere, else. The only thing he looked forward to each week was tutoring English to a Haitian immigrant at a nonprofit agency a few blocks from campus. He had signed up for this as a community service requirement but soon found that he really enjoyed sharing cultural differences with his student, despite their occasional struggles to understand each other.

Unfortunately, his rewarding volunteer experience made his classes and homework seem even duller by comparison. Discouraged and not sure what he should do next, Brandon began to seriously explore college transfer. His father encouraged him to talk to his advisor or a professor he respected about the pros and cons of transfer before making such a major decision.

Brandon met with his advisor, who suggested that he take on a minor in either sociology or cultural studies, both of which would relate to his volunteer work. The advisor also recommended that Brandon look into service learning opportunities in Haiti because he had become so interested in the country and its people. After their talk, Brandon decided not to transfer. Instead he followed his advisor's academic advice and began to plan a spring semester in Haiti.

Parent Perspective

Once they've blazed through freshman year, some college students may begin to feel bored or to experience wanderlust. Like Brandon and Ariel, they may not realize that transfer isn't the only way to deal with these feelings. Parents can help their college student out in several ways:

- Encourage them to look into a self-designed major, ideally one that combines several of their areas of interest
- Propose that they broaden their horizons within the school by joining a club or organization that has a diverse membership and varied activities

- Explore alternate housing options, like joining a fraternity or sorority or moving into a program house. These can offer a livelier, more meaningful living experience
- Suggest that they apply to study abroad or get involved in the college exchange program where they can study at another American university for a semester

REASON TO TRANSFER: PAY ATTENTION, PARENTS

It's tempting to affix the blame for difficulties that students may be experiencing at their new college on parents. However, it's important for the adults in students' lives to make sure that they aren't playing a part in this dynamic by being over- or under-involved with their child's college life.

For students who are used to chafing under their parents' watchful eyes, endless expectations, and restrictions, college offers a chance to finally spread their wings and start exploring some of their own interests on their own timetable. On the other hand, it's not always easy for some mothers and fathers to let go of their sons and daughters. They may continue to exert their influence and be a strong presence in their teen's life in many ways, whether the teen wants them there or not.

Parents who see themselves as "only wanting the best" for their teen or "just trying to be helpful" may feel rejected. Teens, who feel they are perfectly capable of managing their own affairs if only their parents would let them, may feel frustrated and trapped. This dynamic can color the entire collegiate experience if left unchecked.

At the opposite end of the spectrum are parents who believe that, once their child turns eighteen, they're an adult with a completely developed work ethic, sense of responsibility, and understanding of actions and their potential consequences. Unfortunately, nothing could be farther from the truth! Scientific studies show that teens' brains aren't fully developed until their mid-twenties. Expecting a college student to make decisions the way a fifty-year-old would is quite unrealistic.

Colleges are aware of both of these scenarios, which is why they have well-staffed Student Health and Counseling Centers and the FERPA forms available for students to sign. The only problem with this is that some students don't want to avail themselves of either type of support and some parents don't even know the forms exist.

The three scenarios that follow are at the more extreme end of each spectrum, but they offer an inside view of two parent/student situations that could result in transfer, either voluntary or forced.

Scenario 1: Hovering Helicopters

Amanda had grown up hearing about how hard her parents had worked as new immigrants to the United States. They wanted her to take advantage of every opportunity available and had controlled all of her social and academic activities throughout high school. She had played the viola since age five, spoke three languages, was on the high honor roll every semester, and had taken every AP course offered at her private high school. Amanda loved her parents, but it was upsetting when she worked longer and harder than all her classmates and was still criticized for not being perfect.

When Amanda moved into her dorm at a highly selective university in California, her parents pushed her to take the most favorable bed in the room. They preselected her class schedule on the computer to conform to the pre-med major they had chosen for her. The last straw came when her mother stayed in a nearby hotel for two weeks and dropped by her room every day to visit and tidy up.

This was too much for Amanda and her roommates were quickly losing patience with her. She felt like transferring to a school in the middle of nowhere so her mother couldn't check up on her so easily.

At the suggestion of a new friend, Amanda went for counseling at the Student Services Center. Her parents were not pleased when the dean notified them about their daughter's distress. They felt it was not the college's place to interfere. However, the dean persisted in a diplomatic way and Amanda's mother checked out of the hotel that afternoon. Once some of the familial pressure was relieved, Amanda started feeling more at home on campus.

Mothers and fathers may unwillingly recognize a trace of themselves in this vignette. Parents who wonder why their son or daughter keeps talking about transferring to a school that's further away from their hometown when they seem to have the perfect roommate, an ideal class schedule, and plenty of wholesome activities to fill their free time may need to look no further than their own backyard.

Parent Perspective

College should be a time when students separate from their parents and begin to practice the skills and behaviors they've internalized after living with them for eighteen years. Unfortunately, it's impossible to disengage successfully from someone who never leaves you alone! Parents can use these questions to assess their level of involvement with their college student.

- Do you drop in on your son/daughter every single weekend and expect them to spend time with you from dawn to dusk?
- Have you bribed your son/daughter to follow your advice and suggestions by treating him or her to expensive meals or offering to take him or her shopping for clothes or new accessories?
- Are you constantly monitoring his or her course load or study habits?
- Have you been guilty of passing judgment on his or her new friends, professors, or choice of activities?
- Is he or she starting to ignore your texts, phone calls, or emails?

Scenario 2: Their Lips Are Sealed

Nathan had always been a successful and popular kid. No one in his hometown was surprised when he was accepted to every college he applied to. He chose a medium-sized college, not only for its strong academic reputation but for the social emphasis on Greek life.

When Nathan came home for winter break, he talked enthusiastically about his classes, his fraternity, and his girlfriend. To his proud mother and father it sounded like he was excelling in college, just as he had in high school. Alas, nothing could have been further from the truth. Trying to juggle his fraternity's expectations, a roommate who rarely slept and was constantly inviting other kids on the floor over to their room for gaming, and the incessant demands of his high-maintenance girlfriend was taking its toll.

Nathan found himself in the unusual position of doing poorly in all of his classes. Having never experienced failure on any level, he had no idea how to share this with either his advisor or his parents. He chose denial as his coping strategy. Whenever he received a low grade on a paper or exam, he simply ignored it and made plans with his frat brothers or took his girlfriend to the movies.

When he received written notification from the college that he was being placed on academic probation, Nathan refused to panic. "It's fine," he thought to himself. "I'll just need to work harder next semester." Not wanting to worry his parents, he conveniently forgot to mention the notice to them.

Nathan's grades continued to be well below average. Though he appealed the college's decision to expel him for substandard academic performance, he arrived home in May to find an official looking letter rejecting his appeal. No longer an enrolled student at the college and unsure of how to broach the uncomfortable subject to his parents, Nathan simply said nothing.

Parent Perspective

Nathan's mother and father had always been delighted with their oldest son. He was the type of teen that parents never seemed to need to worry about. They expected him to be happy and well adjusted in college and relished hearing stories about his active social life when he was home on break. Somehow they never thought to question that all the stories were about friends. He rarely mentioned his professors, classes, or grades.

A few days after he returned home for the summer break, Nathan's parents received a formal letter from the college informing them that he had been expelled and that his appeal had been denied. They immediately confronted Nathan, who explained that he hadn't wanted to worry them and had thought he could handle the situation himself.

His father contacted a college administrator to try to work something out so Nathan could return in the fall. The school refused to budge. Nathan had been given many chances to raise his grades so there was no other recourse at this point in time. Nathan would either have to reapply to their college or transfer to another school. His father's pleas that they had no idea this was going on fell on deaf ears. "We can't tell you anything because of FERPA," the administrator explained. "Your son never signed a waiver. It was up to him to keep you informed." If these parents could pass along their experience, they would counsel families to:

- Discuss the challenges of balancing Greek life with college-level work before your son or daughter leaves for college
- Talk to your son or daughter about study skills needed for college (books mentioned in the appendix) and resources that he or she may not have had access to in high school, such as writing centers, study groups, and note-taking strategies
- Have your son or daughter sign the FERPA waiver before he or she enters college

Scenario 3: When the Student Knows Best

Occasionally "Student Knows Best" can even trump "Father Knows Best"! Teens may not always be able to articulate their desires clearly or sensibly, but often they really do know their own limitations better than the adults in their lives do.

Haley entered college as a freshman with a negative attitude. She had only been admitted to two of the ten colleges she had applied to so her choices were limited from the start. She really didn't like either of the schools that accepted her, but her parents insisted that she enter college that fall. After dragging her feet, she finally chose the larger university because it had a good biology program.

In the beginning Haley tried to make the best of the situation. She liked her classes and professors and her grades were much better than the ones she had received in high school. But as the semester wore on, she found that the size of the college, the lack of advising support, and the drama queen dynamics of her residence hall were taking an emotional toll on her. Taking some time off or transferring to a new college in the spring seemed like an increasingly attractive option to her.

Haley's phone calls home became litanies of complaints and often ended with either her or her parents slamming down the phone in frustration. Over winter break, she reluctantly agreed to return to school for the spring semester after failing to convince her parents that transferring was her best option.

A month into the new semester, her mother and father received a phone call from the Student Counseling Center. A concerned profes-

sional recommended that they allow Haley to take the rest of the semester off as she was depressed and unable to concentrate on her
studies. Mortified, her parents withdrew her from the college immediately. Haley spent the rest of the semester living at home, working, and
attending regular counseling sessions. That fall she transferred to a new
college that was a much better fit for her.

Parent Perspective

Haley's parents turned a deaf ear to most of her complaints the first
semester. They had been enjoying the freedom of an empty nest and
were not eager to restart the college search process. Her father was also
concerned that she would not get her tuition refunded.

During the winter break, the family had many emotional conversations about transfer. Having their daughter home with them was not the
least bit enjoyable or restful. Haley told them over and over again how
much she hated the college and that she didn't want to go back. Her
parents felt Haley was not sufficiently mature to know what she wanted
or needed and they insisted that she stick with her current college at
least until the end of the year.

Parents can be very resistant to the idea of their son or daughter
delaying entry to college after high school. There is a concern that if
their child doesn't go right away, he or she might end up drifting aimlessly about. If it's an only child or the last child at home, parents may
also be enjoying a "child-free" environment for the first time in years,
which can cloud their judgment.

- Ask yourself if you are pressuring your child into entering a college that they are not happy with. Teens who are forced into an
  experience are often resistant to making the most of the situation.
- Obtain advice from a college counselor regarding nontraditional
  college options such as international or extramural study.
- If the college search does not turn out as the student hoped,
  discuss the option of a work experience or gap year experience
  with the idea that he or she will enter college later.

3

DETERMINING WHAT'S RIGHT FOR YOU

HOW SAVVY ARE YOU ABOUT TRANSFER?

Big concerns for transfer students are credit transfer, financing the remainder of their college education, and finding the best learning environment possible. This section takes a light approach to addressing these serious concerns. So go ahead and take the financial Tic Tac Toe challenge, choose your favorite learning environment through pictures, and answer the credit transfer survey! Don't forget to score yourself in order to identify any potential pitfalls you might face in the transfer process.

Once you have completed the quizzes, you may find that you have more questions about individual schools you're considering transferring to. To get answers, you can go to the college's website or call their admissions office directly.

INTRODUCTION TO TRANSFER PROS AND CONS

The following checklist provides some structure to help compare colleges students may be considering as transfer options. Parts of the checklist you can best research online. For example, if you want to know about a professor's research or books he or she may have written, you will want to go to the college departmental website.

On the other hand, things like lab facilities or housing are best investigated in person. After you have rated each area from 1 to 5, you should total the points for the college under each category to get a subscore for each of the categories, including Quality of Academic Program, Learning Support, Career Placement, Cost, and Location.

Example:
College A
    Quality of Academic Program – 25
    Learning Support – 12
    Career Placement – 15
    Cost – 6
    Location – 15
College B
    Quality of Academic Program – 26
    Learning Support – 6
    Career Placement – 9
    Cost – 8
    Location – 20

Now you can compare colleges using the points in each category. Remember that a higher score is more favorable. Comparing College A and B, we can see that College A has much more learning support and career placement than College B, but the location is less desirable. At this point you can decide what your priorities are in selecting a college for transfer. The student may even want to rate the college they are leaving.

PROS AND CONS CHECKLIST

Students can rate each college that they may transfer to using a five-point rating system for each numbered category (1 = poor, 3 = average, and 5 = outstanding). Compare scores in each category.

Quality of the Academic Program

1. Professors (check out their website for research, publications, and teaching awards)
2. Classes offered (view college catalogue)
3. Facilities (visit facilities relevant to major, that is, general upkeep, lab instruments for scientists, studios for artists)
4. Advising (how does it work? Is there special help for transfers?)
5. Workload (check with tour guides and social media pages)
6. Honors program
7. Library (interlibrary collaborations)

Learning Support

1. Writing center (hours, staffing, location)
2. Tutoring (training, subjects)
3. Available resources (books on CD, learning software)

Career Placement

1. Career center (staffing, hours, types of help)
2. What are recent alums doing now? (statistics)
3. Alumni network (will alums help with internships, shadowing, job search?)
4. Internships, co-op experiences

Cost

1. Cost of Attendance (COA)
2. Financial aid available to transfers
3. Credits that won't transfer

Location

1. Transportation (cost and distance)
2. Surrounding area (recreation, shopping, etc.)
3. Housing (proximity to campus, cost, connection to other transfers)
4. Dining choices
5. Athletic facilities

FAMILY FINANCIAL TIC TAC TOE

Directions: Put a Y in each numbered box matching the question when you answer the question with a yes. Put an N in each numbered box matching the question when you answer no (see figure 3.1).

1. Was your family promised a scholarship at the college that never worked out? Y or N
2. Has your child taken on personal credit card debt? Y or N
3. Is your family employment situation unstable? Y or N
4. Have you drawn up a realistic family budget that includes projected college costs for all children? Y or N
5. Is there a large gap between your estimated family contribution (EFC) and the cost of attending the current college? Y or N
6. Do you have a younger child or children who will begin attending college in the next year or two? Y or N
7. Are transportation costs to and from the campus a strain on your family? Y or N
8. Have you suspended saving for retirement for the time being in order to pay for college? Y or N
9. Are you going through college savings faster than expected? Y or N

- If you have Tic Tac Toe with three Ys in any direction, you need to carefully evaluate whether the colleges your student is considering transferring to are within your family's financial means.
- If you put a Y in any of the boxes, be sure to read the additional cautions below.

1	2	3
4	5	6
7	8	9

Figure 3.1.   Financial Tic Tac Toe

Answer Review: Family Financial Tic Tac Toe

1. Any financial assistance that is promised verbally by athletic coaches or other college officials should not be counted as part of the college budget.
2. Credit card debt should be used as a last resort for college financing because of the high interest rates and fees involved.
3. Work instability is defined here as temporary work, freelancing, or low-income self-employment. Constant ebb and flow in the parents' work situation can lead to serious inaccuracies in financial aid calculations.
4. Maintaining adequate cash flow is extremely important for families entering the college funding years. Budgeting helps ensure that income and expenses are in balance. A realistic budget should include educational costs over the next four years and it should be reviewed annually to incorporate any changes that may have occurred.
5. The EFC may include substantial loans, further burdening the family in the future. Scholarship aid from the original school may not follow the student when he or she transfers, so that should be taken into account.
6. This question also applies to twins, triplets, and step-siblings that may be entering college at the same time.
7. An inflation rate for transportation costs over the four years should be added to your budget. There may also be extra costs associated with travel that you may not have expected, such as limousines or buses to the airport, hotel costs for those driving

long distances, an unexpected rise in fuel costs, or shipping or luggage fees for student possessions.

8. Keep in mind that there is no financial aid for retirement.
9. This includes all money (including 529 plans) that you have put aside for college.

LEARNING ENVIRONMENT PICTURE QUIZ

Do you get excited about writing?

Or do you get excited about hands-on activity?

Do you enjoy reading?

Or do you prefer discussion?

Do you prefer to be graded on individual work?

Or do you prefer to be graded on group projects?

Do you like to know your professors?

Or do you prefer to remain anonymous?

CREDIT TRANSFER SELF-SURVEY

Ask students to rate the following statements as true (T) or false (F) to test their knowledge on credit transfer.

1. A course in which you received a C – is unlikely to transfer.
2. You can receive transfer credit for a remedial course.
3. You are more likely to get transfer credit for an English course than an equine nutrition course.
4. There is no way to receive college credit for military service.
5. In order to receive transfer credit, your institution must be recognized by the American Association of Registrars and Admissions officers.
6. You can receive college credit for religious courses.
7. AP credits will transfer from one college to another.
8. Credits will transfer to fulfill the requirements of your major at your new college.
9. It is easier to transfer credits within a state system of colleges rather than between states or private colleges.
10. On average, students find that nine credit hours don't transfer.
11. The best university official to contact to find out about college transfer is the university registrar.
12. It is helpful to save a course catalogue from your current college.

Credit Transfer Self-Survey Answer Key

1. A course in which you received a C – is unlikely to transfer.
   True – Many colleges require a C or better for transfer credit.
2. You can receive transfer credit for a remedial course.
   False – Generally a remedial course is to refresh your knowledge of material in high school courses for which you will not receive college credit.
3. You are more likely to get transfer credit for an English course than an equine nutrition course.
   True – Colleges only give transfer credit for programs that they offer and few universities offer equine nutrition.

4. There is no way to receive college credit for military service.

   False – Many universities give physical education or health credit for military service.

5. In order to receive transfer credit, your institution must be recognized by the American Association of Registrars and Admissions officers.

   True – This is generally the case.

6. You can receive college credit for religious courses.

   False – Generally you will not receive credit for these unless transferring to an institution of the same religious sect.

7. AP credits will transfer from one college to another.

   Neither true nor false! It depends very much on the institution as to whether they will transfer these credits.

8. Credits will transfer to fulfill the requirements of your major at your new college.

   False – Many times credits will not fulfill major requirements at your new school.

9. It is easier to transfer credits within a state system of colleges rather than between states or private colleges.

   True – There are usually articulation agreements within states that make college credit transfer easier.

10. On average, students find that nine credit hours don't transfer.

    False – On average, about thirteen credit hours won't transfer.

11. The best university official to contact to find out about college transfer is the university registrar.

    True – It is the registrar's office that generally makes the credit decisions.

12. It is helpful to save a course catalogue from your current college.

    True – This can be very helpful in determining course equivalents for credit transfer.

4

HANDS-ON HOMEWORK

TELLING PARENTS

Once a student has decided that college transfer is the best course of action for him or her, the real work begins. For college students, telling the important adults in their lives that they are planning to leave their current college and transfer to a new school can be the hardest part of the process.

When parents first hear that their son or daughter wants to transfer, their initial reaction may be disbelief, distress, or dismay. It may be hard for mothers and fathers to understand why their child wants to leave the "perfect" school the family just spent the last three years searching for. Or they may be indifferent, feeling like they've already done their part and the ball is in the student's court now. The majority of parents usually fall somewhere in the middle.

Parents might be disappointed about a transfer initially, but they are usually willing to be supportive as long as their son or daughter seems motivated to do something besides living at home indefinitely. Students who can share some idea of what their future goals are and their general plan as to how they'll achieve them can also help parents adjust to the idea of changing colleges.

The timing of telling parents about a transfer can greatly influence their reaction. Students handle this discussion in all sorts of ways. Some let their mothers and fathers know well ahead of time or as soon as they return home for a college break so their parents can help them search for an alternate college while they're all under the same roof. During her winter break, Jane described herself as being *"borderline depressed and really stuck."* Though it was a challenge (and scary) for her to have a conversation about transferring with her parents, they were understanding and supportive.

> *"They told me I should spend my break working on applications and trying to write transfer essays. This was good because the questions schools asked like 'Why do you want to transfer?' forced me to be introspective. The answer I wanted to give was 'Because I'm not happy here.' But you can't say that to the Admissions Office! You need to be more focused about what you want to get out of the overall college experience and tell how you would contribute to your new college community."*

Other students choose to wait until the last possible minute to tell their parents they aren't going back to their first college. This doesn't give parents much time to process the news. Not only that, but trying to apply to other colleges—when transfer admission deadlines are looming or have already passed—can create an added level of tension between parents and students.

If the student is transferring because of poor grades or a behavioral issue, mothers' and fathers' initial reactions may be shock or anger that this is the first time they're hearing about a problem. When things weren't going well at her first school, Brittney talked to her older sister about transferring, but didn't tell her parents until she moved back home over the summer. She recalls,

> *"I had only showed them the good grades I got. They had no idea how badly I was doing, that I had failed two classes and got Cs and Ds in some others. I had gone to a professor and told her I was struggling and her response was 'Well, go get some tutoring or something.' So I just stopped going to class. The only reason my parents found out was that I lost my financial aid. They told me I better 'get it together.'"*

Another group of students work on their transfers independently, not telling their families until they've been accepted to a new college or university. Shanna confided in her fiancé, who helped her research schools and organize the information with spreadsheets so she could make the best possible decision for herself.

> *"I wanted to make sure I had a plan in place and was accepted at a new school before I talked to my parents," she says. "I didn't want to jump out of one boat until I was sure I had another one to get into!"*

Regardless of when the decision to transfer is relayed to parents, past transfer students agree that the way the information is conveyed is crucial. Staying calm, showing their parents that they've carefully considered the pros and cons of their decision, and giving specific reasons for the transfer are all good ways to start the conversation. As Jacquie says,

> *"You need to understand that your parents probably won't understand why you want, or need, to transfer. But, if you explain it rationally and logically to them, instead of getting mad or emotional, they'll see that you've really thought about your situation. They'll see that it isn't just an impulsive decision."*

Jacquie sat down and wrote down the reasons why she thought she should stay at her current college and the reasons that she felt she should leave.

> *"This made me realize that all of the reasons on the 'stay' side were fear-based, things like 'What if I never go back to college?' and 'What if I don't have any friends at a new college?' Writing the list legitimized my feelings and by the time I was done, I knew that I really wanted to leave. So I called my mom and very calmly told her about the list and gave her my reasons and then she was able to understand my situation better."*

Parent Perspective

Comprehending why their child wants to change colleges may be difficult for some parents, especially if transfer wasn't part of their own college experience. Initially, they may hope that, if their son or daughter can just make it through freshman year, he or she might change his or her mind.

When her daughter first raised the idea of transferring to a new college after the fall semester of her freshman year seemed to get off to such a good start, Sandy remembers feeling apprehensive.

> "We shared our concerns with her. In my mind I was thinking that maybe things would change second semester. I thought, 'Nobody's really happy freshman year, and they all complain when they come home over Thanksgiving. But, after they've been home for a month at Christmas, they can't wait to get back to school!'"

When her daughter announced her plan to change schools, Valerie remembered her own decision about transferring at the end of her sophomore year of college,

> "I had realized my current school didn't have the major I was interested in. But I ended up switching majors and staying at the college. Then I went on and got a master's in what I really wanted to do. I guess transferring just wasn't part of my culture."

Parents who were transfers themselves may find that the parental role in the transfer process has changed. Vince went on numerous college visits with his son during the transfer process. He observes,

> "Both my wife and I transferred from community college to four-year colleges. That was really different than what we went through with our son. My parents didn't help me at all. I never visited the school, or even the state it was in."

Other mothers and fathers who transferred have positive memories of how their own parents received their news to fall back on. Toby recalls dropping out of college to take a year off. He says he was lucky that his parents were "academic types" with a great belief in education, along with raising kids to be resourceful and independent.

> "My parents were really helpful and that helped me know how to act with my daughter. I knew that I just had to be a sounding board for her. She told me her different ideas and I'd give her my opinion about them. I phrased my advice as the 'pluses and minuses' rather than trying to be forceful or give her directions."

The concern may lie not in the transfer itself but in the school their son or daughter wants to leave or move to. Transferring away from a school that a parent attended can cause family friction, especially if the alumni relationship or family legacy at the college extends back for several generations. Many of these parents are still connected to the college, either through alumni groups, as members of the Parent Association, as class officers, or as generous donors.

A college transfer that parents perceive as lateral or "moving up" might be better received than one they see as "trading down," such as a move from an elite university to a state school that no one but their child seems to have heard of.

Mothers and fathers who are initially reluctant or concerned about their son or daughter going to a college with less name recognition may be surprised by how much they come to appreciate the school their child has selected. It may not be the college or university they imagined, but ultimately students should be in the academic and social setting in which they can be most successful, not the one with the "best" name. Furthermore, if the student's higher education plan is personally designed, he or she is more likely to be committed to it for the long run.

Parents who find themselves feeling anxious about what other parents or family members might say about a lesser-known school should set aside a few minutes to frame their responses to college-related questions they might encounter in social situations. Learning about the new school's history, some of its better-known graduates, or some unique qualities that it has as well as why it's a good match for their son or daughter will make these conversations much easier.

TELLING FRIENDS

Transfers may find that telling their friends about their plans to transfer is almost as nerve-wracking as telling their parents. A commonly voiced concern is that the news won't be well received from friends who are still enthusiastic about the college. Transfers are often afraid of being shunned or ostracized by their peers. They are concerned people will believe they are leaving because the school isn't "good enough" for them. Though this is often untrue, the angst itself is quite real.

Past transfer students were evenly divided on the timing of when to let peers they cared about at their first school know they would be leaving at the end of the semester. Eric remembers the stress of waiting to see if he'd been accepted at the schools he applied to before breaking the news to his freshman friends.

> *"I had to enter the housing lottery at my first school just in case I ended up staying there. I didn't tell any of my friends there what was going on until I was accepted at a different university in June. At that point I was really apprehensive about telling them I was leaving but they were all really supportive about the whole situation."*

Looking back, Jane wishes she had handled telling her friends differently.

> *"I didn't tell my friends at my first school about the transfer (not even my best friend) until I actually got into a new school. A lot of them took it personally. The reason I did it this way was because a girl I knew who transferred told her friends at her first school right away and they shut her out. Now I wish I had been more open with the people that knew me. They would have wanted what was best for me and could have given me extra support."*

WHAT ABOUT A GAP YEAR?

Gap year experiences are sometimes viewed by parents as being synonymous with wealthy teens backpacking aimlessly around Europe. They can be expensive if not carefully planned and executed. However, taking time off can also save families a significant amount of money. This is especially true if the student gains credit hours, work skills, or insight into what he or she would like the future to look like.

The most successful gap years allow students to learn about themselves through some combination of travel, service learning, work, and community college. This type of gap year helps keep down the cost while still allowing for adventurous exploration. Gap years seem to work best when they're structured to give the student an active means of determining strengths and weaknesses, prioritizing goals and ambitions, and turning these into a reality as an adult.

Another common misperception about gap years is that students who take time off during their college years won't be able to graduate on time or that they won't take their studies as seriously. For some college students, taking a semester or a year off before transferring to a new college can make all the difference. This is particularly true for young people who are considering switching to a very different major from the one they started out with or drastically changing their long-term career objectives.

Erica explains how she was able to use her time in between colleges positively and constructively. She began her freshman year of college as a music major, but soon realized that this might not be the career she wanted to pursue.

> "It was really hard to give up being a music student, after I'd spent all of that time auditioning to get into a good music school," she says. "But I left Michigan after winter break and never went back. After I thought about what I wanted to do, it seemed like Arts Management was a career I might be interested in. There was a school in my hometown that offered this as a major so I moved back home and took a class there."

Erica also planned a trip that would immerse her in the world of music and give her another means of comparing business and the arts as career choices.

> "I went to Vienna and tried to get a better perspective on what my feelings were about music. I had the chance to talk to European music students and to see concerts; it was the best experience of my life! I didn't want to rush into anything because, after switching from my first school, I wanted to test the waters before starting at a new college."

The gap year experience can be a challenging and personally rewarding time for many young people. Additionally, it can serve as a great complement to the student's academic coursework and be an excellent addition to his or her resume.

Hannah wanted to earn a college degree but found the academic part of university life draining at times. She discovered a service learning and travel opportunity that gave her a much-needed break while allowing her to stay on track for her college diploma. After leaving her

Canadian college at the conclusion of her sophomore year, Hannah joined AmeriCorps (http://www.nationalservice.gov/programs/ameri corps) for a semester and worked on Arizona Trail Maintenance.

> *"AmeriCorps gave me the chance to leave college, refocus myself, and then go back. That's why I did it twice. The second time was after I'd done two semesters at a New York State university. That time I signed up with AmeriCorps to work on a recycling program in West Virginia. It was a way to broaden my vision of what was possible and to give myself a chance to see what was available outside of the college setting. If you're not exactly sure what you want to do, try a program like this."*

Having a son or daughter take classes at a community college as part of a gap year can raise parents' anxiety levels. They may believe that a four-year degree is the only path to a respectable and rewarding career or that a community college is synonymous with failure or the inability to get into a "real" college. Parents may also be fearful that their child's education and career path will get off track or permanently derailed.

However, sometimes it works to the student's advantage to take some classes at a community college so he or she can stay engaged in higher education, see what other professions might interest him or her, and accrue some credits while gaining more of a sense of direction through active self-reflection.

COMMUNITY COLLEGE OPTIONS

Transfer to community college from a four-year college has become an increasingly popular option. Attending community college (even for one course) is quite common for students who now have bachelor's degrees. In the 2013–14 academic year, about 46 percent of students who graduated from a four-year college had attended community college at some point (National Student Clearing House, Research Center, 2015).

Ten years ago most transfers went from community college to a four-year college, but as the cost of college has continued to rise well above the rate of inflation, community college has become a more at- tractive choice among students unhappy with their first college. Freshman enrollment has also increased at many community colleges over the last decade.

Community College: A Bridge to Another Four-Year College

A number of students have said that transferring to community college has been a good experience for them after attending a university that was a poor match. Sometimes students were not happy in college because the major that they thought they wanted turned out to be unappealing or they couldn't find a major that interested them. At this point, several students said that it was important to find their focus by sampling a lot of different classes and they could do this at a lower cost in community college.

Transferring from a four-year college to a community college does not necessarily mean that all the classes are easier. The difficulty of the class depends a lot on the particular community college, the professor teaching the class, and the difficulty of the subject matter. Classes in genetics, statistics, and calculus are conceptually difficult, which means that they will be challenging in a community college. Some students who have taken honors classes at a community college have even found them more difficult than those at the local state school.

Entering a community college in the spring can be challenging for those students interested in courses with prerequisites that are only taught in the fall. Students need to pay attention to course sequences and prerequisites for classes that they wish to take. The most common sequences of classes occur in mathematics, biology, chemistry, and physics. Getting out of sync can result in an extra semester or even an extra year of college. Sometimes students can get back on track by doubling up on classes, which is not ideal, or taking the prerequisite online.

Taking classes at a local community college in the summer is useful for students who have a really demanding course load at their university but still want to graduate in four years. These students sometimes decided to change their major late in their academic life or they are trying to achieve a dual major. Pre-med and pre-vet students also use this strategy to try to complete all of the requirements to enter graduate school.

Students may choose to attend a community college for a specialized major that they are interested in. Some of the top majors at community colleges include:

- Registered Nursing
- Homeland Security/Criminal Justice
- Licensed Practical Nursing
- Radiology
- Computer technologies

Attending community college is a confidence builder for students who have left a four-year college experience for academic reasons. These academic difficulties have many different causes. The academic and social pressures of college may exacerbate mental health or addiction issues. Sometimes the student is just in the wrong major or social environment, causing a downward spiral in grades.

Many of these young adults *feel* as though they have failed for the first time in their lives and they need to recover from that experience. Taking classes at a community college can be an important bridge to recovery and progress.

For students who have trouble with time management, doing well in a few classes can help them step up to a more demanding schedule. Many of these colleges have extra services and even remedial classes to help students improve their skills. Several individuals who ultimately transferred to a university mentioned that they felt like they got back on track by getting good grades in community college classes.

Financial Choice in Community College

Families like the fact that they will know what community college is going to cost when they are considering it because tuition and fees are published each year. The financial aid for community college is a small piece of the financial picture, so families don't have to guess at what their obligation will be.

Students are often able to fit a work schedule around the classes offered at a two-year college, which can reduce their financial obligation even more. In addition, students who are not prepared for college-level work can take remedial classes or a reduced class schedule in order to make the academic workload more manageable.

Clearly, if the student lives at home, that can save a lot of money. This is not always practical, especially if the community college is not close to home and if the transportation links are poor. In addition, there may be labs or discussion groups in the evening that would require multiple trips to campus. Some two-year colleges have dorms, but many require the students to live off campus. Families need to consider the cost of the nearby rental market or the cost of commuting by car when they figure the total cost of attendance at the college.

Transferring from Community College to a Four-Year College

Entering community college can seem like a relaxed and low-key choice at first because the admissions process is less taxing than the one required for four-year institutions. Freshmen may not know if they will finish with an associate's degree or go on for a bachelor's degree, but they still need good advising.

Over 60 percent of community college students initially plan to transfer to a four-year college, but a much lower percentage actually makes the transition. According to NISTS (National Institute for the Study of Transfer Students), good advising, faculty mentoring, and family support all help students reach for a bachelor's degree.

Developing an academic plan at the beginning of college is very important even if it changes over the years. Freshmen are usually assigned an academic advisor at the beginning of school, but if they don't communicate well with that person they need to seek out an advisor that they connect with. The financial advantage of community college disappears if the student ends up taking a lot of extra classes that won't lead to a degree or won't transfer.

Having an academic plan with a goal in mind is the most efficient use of a student's time and money. Yet one of the attractions of community college is the ability to sample from lots of different disciplines at a lower cost if the student has no idea what he or she wants to major in. This can take a lot of time and the cost is not insignificant. Students who have no direction have the option of using college career services and taking advantage of the career counselors and surveys that they provide to help achieve an academic focus.

There is one exception to the rule that attending community college followed by transfer to a public university is the least expensive option. Students who did well in high school are attractive to private colleges that have significant funding set aside to attract talented freshmen. In general, the financial aid for freshmen is much more generous at private colleges than it is for transfers. This means that a talented student who started at a private college may actually have a lower cost of attendance over four years than one who transferred from community college.

Credit Transfer in Community College

Students who know that they want to go on for a four-year degree should begin mapping out that path immediately as they enter community college. Community colleges have agreements for credit transfer with specific four-year colleges (articulation agreements) that make the process much easier. Some states (for example, New York and California) that have a large number of community colleges and state universities have many of these agreements already worked out.

Credit transfer is nonstandard in many states. Students who are unsure about credit transfer in their state and that have a goal of attending a particular university should contact the registrar at that institution as soon as possible in order to obtain their policies about credit transfer. They should also print out the description of the courses they are taking and keep the syllabi in order to be able to advocate for receiving credit at the four-year college.

Reverse Transfer

It is a problem in terms of career placement and advancement if students transfer from community college, earn credits at a four-year college, and then leave without a degree. According to a study by NISTS, over a million people currently have over sixty credits (average number to obtain an associate's degree) from various colleges, yet have no degree.

Some community colleges are developing reverse transfer agreements with universities in their state to deal with this problem by awarding associate's degrees after transfer based on the additional college-level work at the four-year institution.

Community College and the Traditional College Experience

Over time some two-year colleges have changed to become more like four-year colleges as they have added more athletic teams and residence halls for students. An athlete who really wants to continue playing his or her sport may want to consider community college as an additional option because less than 6 percent of high school athletes have the opportunity to play in college according to the NCAA (National Collegiate Athletic Association).

Community colleges have begun recruiting athletes for their teams that live outside the area. They are also accepting more international students that require housing. In the 2014–15 academic year, there were over seventy thousand international students enrolled in community college. These are two of the factors behind the construction of community college dormitories.

In addition, some students really want the experience of living in a dormitory with lots of other young people their age that come from different backgrounds. Some community colleges have responded to this desire and built residence halls, although many of their peers remain commuter schools.

Academic Quality of Community Colleges

Community colleges vary a lot in academic quality. The two-year college that is nearest the family home may not be the one that best fits the needs of the student. Not every community college offers the same majors, for example. When evaluating the college, students should look at the graduation rate, which is a good indicator of whether the institution lets students flounder. If it is below 30 percent, it is a cause for concern.

Attracting good students is important to one group of community colleges that is making a concerted effort to offer honors courses that are more challenging. This group of colleges can be found at the honor council website www.nchchonors.org.

Pre-professional fields like physical therapy and medicine require rigorous preparation in order to be well prepared for graduate entrance exams. This presents a dilemma for the student at community colleges, where the professors develop their curriculum for the average student because they have such a broad range of students in their classes. Easy science classes will not give these students the proper preparation. If no honors science classes are offered, the ambitious pre-med student may choose to take them during the summer at another institution.

Community colleges now fill many roles in the educational journey of students. No longer just local commuter schools, they have evolved to meet the needs of many different types of students. Today, students from all different backgrounds attend, including athletes, international students, gap year students, students in recovery, students looking for particular majors, and transfers from four-year institutions.

5

ALL ABOUT COLLEGE VISITS

WHY VISIT?

Just how vital is it for students to see the colleges they're considering transferring to beforehand? Doing research or visiting student- or college-based groups online to get a feel for the school is a great idea in terms of finding out general information about a school. Still, there are certain aspects of a college or university that simply can't be conveyed on a computer or phone screen. When Kasey transferred colleges the first time, she admits that she didn't have a realistic understanding of what being a student at that particular school would be like.

> "If I had taken the time to research the college and visited it as a [potential] transfer student, rather than just socially for basketball games on campus, I think I would have realized that it wasn't a good fit for me. I didn't do an official campus tour, or meet with the admissions department or the professors in my major, or even try to do an overnight with an enrolled student. All of these would have showed me that it wasn't the college for me. The campus was beautiful, but I didn't understand what moving from a public to a private university would mean in terms of my overall education."

Though transfers may not feel like taking a tour or going to an admissions meeting like they did as a high school student, that doesn't mean they should scrap the visit entirely. A number of colleges now have freshman open houses that include special sections for transfer students. Others hold separate Transfer Open Houses or Transfer Days that allow potential transfers to immerse themselves in all the school has to offer.

Seeing a college in "real life" can give potential transfers an entirely different mental picture of the school than the one gained by reviewing the college's website. Additionally, many of the questions potential transfers have are better answered informally and in person, either by students currently enrolled in the program of study the transfer is considering, by professors or a department head within their major, or by an admissions or transfer counselor.

Students are also quite resourceful when it comes to arranging overnight or day visits with people they know who currently attend a college they're considering transferring to instead of going through the college's admissions office. Marjorie, whose son transferred when his major was eliminated at his first university, is a big fan of this type of college visit.

> "It's very important to visit the school you're considering transferring to and to talk to the students and professors there informally instead of just relying on the organized tours. My son actually spent the day there with a friend from his summer music camp who was also majoring in engineering. That gave him a really good feel for the school."

Walking around a campus gives potential transfers a wealth of impressions that may ultimately influence their final transfer decision. Visits make it easier to assess the college's size, layout, and the physical condition of the school's buildings. According to Alec, who chose not to visit the college he transferred to the spring of his freshman year,

> "On their website they show pictures of the nicest places on campus, like the beautiful view from one spot, a really nice looking building, and one of the new dorms. You don't see the south side of campus and that's where I was stuck!"

College visits allow transfers to get a glimpse of what the campus social atmosphere is like, including how the other students and faculty dress, talk, and act. Wandering around the school, eating in the dining hall, visiting the fitness center, or sitting in on a class are all ways to get a sense of how comfortable a school would be for a transfer student.

Assessing the level of campus safety is important too, especially for the peace of mind it can bring to both students and their families. Colleges and universities located in higher-risk areas may send frequent (or occasional) alerts to students about streets or parts of town they should avoid at particular times. This can be disconcerting and unsettling for students, especially if they have night classes. Students in rural or remote areas may also be fearful about venturing out of their dorm during certain times of day or night.

Determining the atmosphere of the town or city the college is located near is also easier in person. The first time Gray and her mother visited the northeastern college she was transferring to was during Transfer Orientation Week. Gray found the campus safe and welcoming, with a focus on diversity and making sure all the students felt at home. The affluent town the school was located in was a different story.

> *"I grew up poor, not around a lot of suits and yoga moms," she says candidly. "That town was the only place I was ever yelled at for being queer when I walked down the street with my partner. And I grew up in the South."*

LGBTQ college students (and their parents/guardians) expect institutions of higher learning to be more sensitive to their needs. Like Gray's second school, many colleges and universities have responded to this by increasing their level of services and improving their campus climates. However, it's important to note that these changes do not always extend off campus to the local community.

Given the vast differences in climate and weather conditions across the United States, the timing of a college visit can be important. Many prospective students choose to visit colleges during the nicer months. It may come as an unpleasant shock when winter arrives, with its many varieties of precipitation and rapid temperature changes.

For other students, some regions of the country are too hot and dry in the spring and summer months. Extreme weather conditions like flooding, tornados, or blizzards can also be difficult for students to adapt to. Planning a college visit during the least temperate time of year may be advisable!

TIPS FOR TRANSFER VISITS

- Visit the college as if you know nothing about it (even if it's a campus you've spent time on before).
- Speak up! Ask questions wherever you go.
- Sit in on at least one class in your major. Take a lesson with your potential teacher, practice with the team, or attend a club meeting.
- Ask to shadow a student in your major for the day. Eat meals with them and meet their friends.
- See if the college allows potential transfers to have overnight visits with current students.

College visits are one way parents can be useful to their son or daughter, both as a sounding board and a second set of eyes. Parents who are concerned about a negative experience that their child had at their previous school may want to see the college or university and gather all the facts about it with their son or daughter.

WHY NOT VISIT?

Given all this, why would a transfer student choose *not* to visit a prospective college? For some, trying to juggle their current college's workload and maintain their grades while filling out the transfer paperwork, requesting credit evaluations, and writing the personal essays required in the transfer process leaves little time for planning visits to other colleges.

For others, the physical distance and transportation costs involved in visiting the schools they're considering transferring to is just too much. Daniel was attending a Minnesota college when he decided it would be better for his career goals to pursue his music major at a Texas university.

> *"I went there cold," he admits about his decision to transfer without visiting beforehand. "I told myself I could adapt to anything. I had no idea what I was getting into. I just put everything in my hatchback and drove south."*

Daniel did need to adjust to some things at his new school. However, the fact that it was affordable and had an excellent music program made his transfer worth any difficulties he had to cope with.

Students might refuse to visit a college or university in their hometown because they have preconceived (usually negative) notions about the school. Visiting the campus the same way they would an out-of-area school can either validate their concerns or replace their misconceptions with a more realistic view of the school, the professors, and the type of students that go there.

Transfers who are returning to their original college after spending a year or two somewhere else may not feel a need to revisit the campus. Instead they prefer to focus on what needs to change for them the second time around to ensure a successful undergraduate experience. This could mean taking more, less, or different classes. Other returning transfers get a job, join a new activity or club, or try a different style of housing.

Transfer students may have a friend or relative who attends, or attended, a college they're interested in transferring to. Having spent time on the campus previously, it may feel familiar enough that they don't feel the need to visit. Students may also end up transferring to a college where their parents work. After living in close proximity to the school while growing up, they may already have a positive impression of it. Sometimes there is a financial incentive for family members of the college's employees to attend the school that is just too good to pass up. Finally, for some transfers, being closer to their hometown and already established friend community is appealing.

Parent Perspective

Like students, parents may not believe that a college visit is necessary because their child has already spent time at the school visiting the friends or relatives who either went there or who live in the area. Other parents encourage their son or daughter to reapply to a college or university he or she was interested in (and visited in high school) but didn't get accepted to.

If the school isn't easily accessible, the family may wait until their son or daughter has been admitted before planning a trip there. Or they may choose not to visit at all. This decision may have unexpected repercussions. In today's digital age, where things are just a click away, physical distance may not seem like a big deal. But the difference between virtual and real miles can be huge.

Mark's son decided to transfer to a university located in a city at the opposite end of the country from his hometown. His parents had never been there and had no idea how his moving hundreds of miles away would impact them as a family.

"We wish he was closer," Mark admits, noting that it's a long, tough drive from New Jersey to Louisiana. Air travel isn't much better; it's expensive and the flights usually involve multiple transfers and long layovers.

Parents of transfers also discovered that unforeseen costs of long-distance travel, like car or van rentals, meals and lodging, and gas, can quickly add up. Long-distance logistics can be tough for mothers and fathers too. However, often the hardest part of being separated by a significant distance is less tangible. In high school, parents may have become accustomed to being able to attend their child's band concerts, football and soccer games, theater performances, and academic honor ceremonies. This may change when they're hundreds of miles apart. *"We can't always be there to be part of his accomplishments,"* Mark says regretfully.

Marjorie's son's first college was in Missouri. She recalls getting there to be "sort of a big deal" in terms of visits and school breaks. As her son began researching transfer, she and her husband requested that he focus on schools in their home state of Massachusetts the second time around. She adds,

> *"We were used to being able to go to all of his concerts but, because of the distance, my husband only made it to one and I flew out in the spring to see another one. Now that he's back in the area, we can go to all of them together."*

VISITS AND INTERNATIONAL TRANSFERS

Planning a visit before transferring to an American college can be difficult, if not impossible, for international students. They will need to be even more vigilant about vetting the college ahead of time by using a variety of online and offline resources, such as:

- Checking out the college or university's website, particularly its design and usability
- Googling the school's reviews to see comments others have made online about it
- Reviewing different schools' rankings (from a reputable source) while keeping in mind that what majors are offered there may actually be the more important factor
- Joining Facebook groups for current students (U.S. and international) at the college, as well as for the class the transfer would be graduating
- Requesting paper materials like brochures and course catalogues from the Admissions Office
- Connecting with the college's international transfer advisors ahead of time
- Talking to friends or relatives from home who have successfully transferred to an American college about their experiences and perceptions
- Contacting alumni with specific questions about the school. Some colleges have alumni clubs in major cities overseas and the members can provide input about what it was like to be an international student in an American university
- Researching the climate of the state where the college or university is located
- Determining the social culture of the college and town/city. A deciding factor between two colleges might well be whether there is a diversity of people, foods and restaurants, and recreational opportunities nearby
- Making sure there are clubs and services that are specifically geared to international transfer students

QUESTIONS FOR STUDENTS TO ASK BEFORE TRANSFERRING

Potential transfers should gather as much information and as many impressions as they can during their college visit(s). Based on their prior college experience, students may have a number of specific questions for the college they're visiting or actively communicating with.

Compiling a list of things they want to learn about the school before committing to transferring there will help students decide if it will be a better fit for them than their previous school. Some answers may be more important to students. Others will be equally important to their parents.

Credit Transfer

Parents agree that the more goal-directed and organized their son or daughter is about making sure he or she can transfer the maximum number of credits to the new school, the better off he or she will fare in terms of being able to graduate on schedule.

What can be less clear to families is the direct link between credit transfer and the final cost of college. Credits that are required to graduate (such as religion or physical education) or that don't transfer toward the student's major may need to be made up in the summer or during the school year at an additional cost to the family.

Sample Questions

- Is there someone at the college that I can meet with before the academic year begins to help me maximize my credit transfer so I won't be behind everyone else in my major?
- Do you accept AP scores from high school?
- Are there any specific graduation requirements that will have to be filled at this college before I can graduate?
- Will any/all of my transferred credits count toward my major or minor? If they don't, can they be applied to General Education or used as elective credits?
- Should I bring course catalogues or syllabi of classes from my previous school for my new advisor to review?
- Are summer classes available through the college or a community college if I need them to complete my degree on time?

The Cost of College Transfer

Students who want to transfer don't always understand the impact that a change in tuition payments can have on the family budget or the long-term effect that accumulated college debt might have on their own fiscal future. No matter how much legwork your son or daughter has done to initiate transfer, finances are one area where parental input is essential.

College transfer often means a loss of any scholarships or grants the student might have been receiving from the initial college. This can be challenging for parents, especially when the transfer involves a significant increase in tuition or if the family has more than one child in college concurrently.

Sample Questions

- Is there someone in the Financial Aid Office at the college who can help me fill out financial aid forms?
- Will any scholarships I'm receiving now transfer with me?
- Do you have any special scholarships for transfer students at your school? Will I need to meet certain requirements to be eligible for them?
- Can state scholarships be used at this school? Do these have residency requirements?
- How much will I have to pay for items like transportation, textbooks, or necessary technology?
- How much has tuition increased over the past few years? Is this a trend you expect to see continue in the upcoming years?
- What will the net cost of attendance (taking credit transfer, scholarships, and work study or other employment into account) at this school be per year?

Academic and Career Goals

A change in colleges frequently involves an adjustment in transfers' academic outlook and timetables. Asking what academic support services are available (transfer-specific and general) during the college visit is highly recommended. If the student is trying to get admitted into a "specialty program" (nursing, engineering, or business, for example), it's also important to clarify if he or she will be admitted directly to that department or if he or she has to start as a general or undeclared major and then apply to the preferred program of study.

Classwork is the foundation of a college education, but in today's job market gaining hands-on experience through internships or co-ops is equally valuable and can often lead to a job offer right out of college. Part of a college or university's role is helping students take steps toward meeting their future professional goals. Asking questions about how the school plans to do this during a college visit can be reassuring to students (and their parents!).

Sample Questions

- What is the course load like for transfers? Will the number of credits I have to take per semester be significantly higher than what others in my major are carrying?
- Will my class schedule leave time for me to join clubs and have a social life? Or will I be stuck in the library every weekend?
- As a transfer student, will opportunities like studying abroad, co-ops, and internships be available? Are these paid? Are they highly competitive?
- What academic support services does the college offer to transfer students (individual tutoring or group review sessions)?
- Where did the faculty in my major attend college and what is their degree in? Have they been published? Are the deans and faculty full time? How much time do they spend teaching classes?
- Are professors willing to meet with transfer students if they require extra help to catch up with the rest of the class, particularly in courses related to their major?
- How do I connect with my academic advisor? How often are we required to meet?
- What is the college's retention rate? How many years does it take the average student to graduate?

Career Counseling and Job Placement Services

With a fluctuating economy and uncertain job market, parents may have concerns about their child's future once they've completed college. Understanding the college or university's long- and short-term commitment to preparing their son or daughter for employment or graduate school is important. Parents may want to suggest that they be allowed to add a few questions to the list based on their own employment experiences over the years.

Sample Questions

- What type of career counseling does the school provide to students?
- Is career counseling available to recent graduates too? How long after I graduate would I be able to take advantage of this service?
- Do you have pre-professional advisors for programs like medicine, law, and business?

Colleges and universities with strong alumni groups or other professional organizations can offer college students many advantages in terms of advice, support, and future networking opportunities.

Sample Questions

- Does the college have an alumni association?
- Are special alumni events held throughout the year?
- How many alumni are actively involved with the college on a regular basis?
- Are your alumni willing to help link students with internships, interviews, or job opportunities in their field?

Housing for Transfers

Students will want to spend time in their room while at college, sleeping, studying, or just relaxing, so seeing what types of housing the college offers transfers is important. Housing preferences for transfer students are as diverse as the students themselves. For some, living in a college dorm is the best place to meet other students. Others find college housing too confining or the other students too immature for them.

Parents should keep in mind that a living situation that's ideal for one transfer student may drive another crazy. Students are probably the best judge of what living arrangement will work best for them.

Sample Questions

- Is campus housing guaranteed for transfer students? Is the housing deposit refundable?
- Are transfer students required to live in residence halls with freshmen?
- Is there a "transfer house" or "transfer dorm" that only transfer students live in?
- Are transfer students expected to find their own off-campus housing or is that something Residence Life helps with?
- Do dorms have a key or keyless entry system? How are the residence halls monitored?
- What is the college's policy on overnight or weekend guests? How many visitors are allowed at a time and how long can they stay in the dorm?
- Do the dorms have a kitchen that students can use?

College Life

The number one concern for transfer students during a college visit is often "Will I be able to make friends here?" Walking around the campus during a visit and observing how the students interact with each other and what pastimes they're engaging in will help students assess this.

Don't forget to take time to determine what resources and activities are available off campus too. Potential transfers may also want to find out more about how and where students at the college spend their free time and money. Exploring the college's way of life is definitely a place where the student should take the lead. Parents may be interested in how their son or daughter will be spending his or her free time, but students are the ones who will actually be making those decisions on a daily basis.

Sample Questions

- Is this school a "suitcase college," where the majority of students live locally and go home every weekend?

- Where is the best place to meet people? How many student clubs and activities are there? Are there things to do in the town or city for students?
- How safe is your school? Do you have twenty-four-hour campus security or "escort" services?
- What type of health and mental health support services does the college offer to transfer students (counseling, support groups, health clinic)?
- Is the health clinic open twenty-four hours a day? How far away is the nearest hospital?
- What are the hours for the closest pharmacy? Do they deliver or do students need to pick up their medications in person?
- What are the dining plan options for transfers? Are you allowed to opt out? Does the school have "flex dollars" or another similar program?
- Does the dining hall offer foods for students with dietary restrictions (for example, Crohn's disease, diabetes, or lactose intolerance)?
- What types of sporting events are popular here? How much do tickets cost? Is it hard to get them?
- Are there work study jobs or do transfers need to find their own employment?
- Are students allowed to have cars on campus? What's the availability and cost of parking a car there?
- Is there regular transportation between the town/city and campus? What types of transportation are available when it's time to go home for breaks? Do their arrival and departure times coincide with the college schedule?

FOR INTERNATIONAL TRANSFERS

- What countries do most of the college's transfer students come from?
- Will I need to pay full tuition? Is there financial aid or scholarships available to out-of-country college students?
- What international requirements will I need to fulfill to come to this college (for example, Test of English as a Foreign Language)? Once I

arrive on campus will there be resources to help me improve my English language skills?

- As an international transfer, will I have enough time to get to know my professors so I can get employment or graduate school recommendations from them?
- Do I need an international credit evaluation service?
- Are there any extra types of academic supports available for international students?
- Will I live with another international or American transfer student? Or will I live with someone who has been at the school since their freshman year?
- Are there any clubs or organizations at the college that are specifically geared toward international students?
- Who will I be able to turn to if I have a medical emergency or some other type of crisis (if no relative or friend is available)?
- Do the dorms close down over school breaks/holidays? Will the college help me find alternate housing during those times or will I need to do that myself?

6

PARENTS TALK ABOUT
COLLEGE TRANSFER

OVERVIEW

College students are in a period of transition, caught between the adolescents they were and the adults they'll soon become. When teens experience a problem during college, they are frequently torn between trying to act grownup by handling it themselves or wanting their parents to step in and make it all better for them.

Parents find themselves in a similar predicament. Though they're no longer in charge of all aspects of their offspring's lives, they still want to help him or her make good decisions and wise choices. One of the hardest parts of being the parent of a transfer student is trying to figure out how much or how little involvement to have with the process.

Patience Pays Off

Parents may intuitively sense that something isn't quite right with their son or daughter and that he or she is struggling emotionally or academically at the new college. This feeling of unease can be further compounded by a lack of familiarity with the campus, coursework, other students, and the academic faculty and college administration. There can also be a natural inclination to deny or ignore "red flags" after all the effort involved in getting a teen safely settled in the college of his or her choice.

Valerie and her husband hired an independent college consultant to help their family begin the college search process. Together they came up with a list of colleges to visit, fourteen of which their daughter applied to. When their daughter announced that she was leaving the private California college that they had all considered a perfect fit for her to take classes at a community college in Colorado, Valerie admits she was "somewhat surprised" by the drastic shift in plans.

> "My initial response was 'No way!' I was afraid that if she stopped going to college she wouldn't ever go back. I felt very strongly about her getting a four-year college degree. We value education and when you're in college it's a magic four years. You're surrounded by all these people you have things in common with, you're exposed to the liberal arts, and you learn things you'll need to know as an educated adult so you can hold intelligent conversations with others."

Despite her concerns, Valerie listened to her daughter's reasons for wanting to leave California.

> "It seemed like she, not the school, changed. She had been spending her summers working in Colorado and she decided that she didn't like all the California traffic or the people or the environment there. It's hard to be an outdoors person in Los Angeles. And the driving and all of the road rage she saw really got to her. She said all the people there were crabby and never smiled."

After further discussion, Valerie and her husband agreed to support their daughter's transfer to a state university in Colorado. Then she took a step back.

> "I told her that if she really wanted to do this then she'd have to do the research, figure out how to apply for transfer, and handle it herself. She's a very organized person and she did it."

Valerie has no qualms about the way the family handled the transfer, although it wasn't always easy. She sometimes wonders if her daughter regrets her decision but readily acknowledges that it was hers to make.

Other students will need time to process their experience at the previous college by talking with family, friends, or a professional counselor. Some regroup by enrolling in classes, working, or engaging in a service learning or volunteer opportunity. Even though these aren't formal education, when intentionally structured, they are excellent ways for students to learn practical skills or more about themselves prior to reentering a four-year college or university.

Toby's daughter had an uneven first year at the elite Massachusetts college she attended. He recalls that she quickly made some close friends and joined various activities. But she also had a roommate with mental health issues and was put on academic probation, though school had always been easy for her. When his daughter told him she would be leaving the college at the end of the year, Toby acknowledges that he wasn't sure how she reached her decision.

Given this, he didn't object when she took some time in between colleges to figure out what to do next.

> "If your kid wants to transfer, they should do the footwork themselves. If they can't do that then they should take time off to work or do something constructive until they are ready to make the transfer happen," he says. "She ended up becoming part of World Wide Opportunities on Organic Farms in Hawaii and lived there for several years, working on different farms. She did well there but eventually realized that 'trustafarians' (trust-fund hippies) were a strange culture without much of a future. At that point she discovered the Eco-League, a consortium of small, alternative colleges in different states."

Attracted by the agro-ecology major that a college in Arizona offered, his daughter initiated her transfer there with minimal input from Toby. Though he wishes she had visited a few more eco-colleges before making her final decision, Toby concedes that she did the research beforehand and knew she wanted to be in a warm place that was used to dealing with nontraditional students. Best of all, she now has an undergraduate degree from the college!

Communication Counts

For parents of college students, it can be really difficult to know when to ask questions, when to be supportive but let their son or daughter resolve the issue, or when to intervene. The best way parents can help when their college student begins to talk about transfer is to check in with him or her on a regular basis, either in person, by phone, or through social media.

If questions are asked in a genuinely curious and caring way rather than by trying to pry information out of them or passing judgment, students will probably appreciate the support and be more willing to openly discuss any issues they're having.

For some college students, articulating why they want to transfer is easy. The reasons may not be ones their parents agree with, but at least there's a place to begin the discussion. Other students present as deeply distressed but are unable to say anything other than "It isn't working," "It's not a good fit for me," or "I hate it here."

Though no parent wants to see their child depressed or struggling, this can be frustrating for mothers and fathers. This is especially true when the college experience seemed to get off to a great start and there is no apparent reason for their child's anguish. Understand that some kids truly don't know why they are so unhappy or what they want to do next. If they aren't happy where they are but can't seem to figure out what they'd rather be doing, they should be persuaded to slow down the transfer process.

> *"They should be able to give you concrete reasons about why they want to transfer so you know it isn't just an impulsive decision on their part. Have them think about and articulate what they're looking for so they can be sure not to make the same mistake again. Then you have to really listen to what your son or daughter is saying and try to respect that," explains Debbie, the mother of a transfer student.*

For some parents, communicating about college expectations with a son or daughter who has a different personality structure than theirs can be tough in the best of times, let alone when college transfer is involved. Tom notes that he and his daughter were probably equally frustrated at times during her transfer process.

> *"We have different styles of relating to things. My analytical personality versus her emotional one was a struggle. I figured she needed to find something she'd be happy with so when she mentioned something of interest, I'd help her research it to see what kind of jobs were in that field and how they paid. But she didn't really want my advice."*

In some cases, education professionals may recommend that families take the Myers-Briggs Type Indicator (MBTI), a questionnaire that shows how people perceive the world around them and how they make their decisions. This may help neutralize the conflicts that can arise in stressful situations like a college transfer.

Being aware of how the other person is processing information can also help adults and students understand each other better. With this frequently comes the realization that the other person isn't doing things purposefully or maliciously. It's just how they're wired internally. The MBTI encourages parents and their kids to value each other's different perspectives instead of thinking things like "She is making me crazy with all that nagging!" or "Look at what he did now. What is wrong with him?"

As the transfer progresses, communication can become strained when a parent and a student have noticeably dissimilar ways of approaching specific tasks and deadlines. When they first decide to transfer, college students frequently take the initiative to get the process started. Once students have been accepted to a new school, parents may notice a lack of urgency about accomplishing the remaining tasks associated with their transfer (such as getting a physical or submitting required forms).

For adults used to accomplishing tasks in a timely way, this relaxed attitude can be both exasperating and worrisome. College students do not usually welcome frequent reminders or anxious questions about progress being made. Therefore it's best to talk about the transfer process calmly, without taking over the conversation. Let the student take the lead and then deal with any consequences that may arise from his or her decisions.

Money Matters

When a student changes colleges, the family financial contribution toward his or her education is likely to alter as well. Tuition payments may increase and scholarships can magically disappear. Depending on how many credits transfer to the new college or university, the student's graduation date may be extended or he or she may need to cram extra courses into each semester in order to walk down the aisle with the rest of the class. Both of these will require an additional financial commitment.

Luckily, some students transfer between colleges or universities with similar, or even lower, fee structures. But others will be looking at a drastic increase in annual tuition fees. Making sure transfer students understand the cost differential between the college they're currently enrolled in and the one(s) they're hoping to transfer to is definitely a parental responsibility. Mark and his wife openly discussed the financial implications of their son's transfer with him beforehand.

> "When we learned that the transfer college would be two times the price of the first university (which wasn't cheap either), we reminded him that we would pay for four years of college and after that it was on him. . . . He worked his way through college, partly because he knew how much it was costing us. That made him grow up a lot."

Talking about money with a son or daughter can be the toughest part of the college transfer for parents. Parents may feel guilty or embarrassed when they have to tell their child that the college they want to transfer to is just too expensive. Vince, whose son transferred from a rural state school to a large Midwestern university, advises,

> "Understanding your family's financial situation before you get involved with a college is very important, especially if you have more than one child in college. Not everyone is capable of affording the school their kid wants."

Susan, a financial advisor and mother of two college graduates, agrees that discussing money honestly can feel like a taboo subject to many people.

> "Some parents will talk like they never have any money and others will say things like 'Hang the consequences. We'll just go for it!' Both of these are mixed messages and are one of the reasons that our country has over 43 billion dollars' worth of college debt," she says.

For parents that began the discussion about college affordability in high school, transfer merely reinforces what was already talked about and understood by everyone involved. Tom addressed finances with his son and daughter before the first college application was even begun.

"My wife and I talked to both our kids about what our financial commitment would be and how long it would last for. That way when they chose colleges to apply to, they would understand which schools would be in their reach financially. We told our kids we'd pay half of the tuition, up to $10,000/year for their undergraduate college and they would be responsible for the rest. Our view is that they're more invested in something they help pay for."

For those who didn't discuss money the first time around, college transfer can open the door to a realistic assessment of family finances and how these relate to higher education. When the adults involved are on the same page and have put some thought into balancing what their financial capability and monetary obligation to their son or daughter are, this talk will go smoothly. By the end of it, students should have all the information they need to decide if the cost of the school(s) they're interested in and the debt they could amass through student loans is worth the education and degree they'd receive.

A large or unexpected tuition increase may also cause families to question whether the college is worth it. If finances become a problem, parents and students might need to assess factors like whether the student would be just as happy at a college with lower tuition, especially if the student isn't able to work during the semester for academic reasons or if they can't find a summer job to help them offset college costs.

There is one other thing parents should keep on their radar. Because colleges commit to their financial aid budget at fixed times of the year, they aren't always able to adapt quickly to a change in family finances. If a parent loses his or her job or becomes disabled or another family member has an unforeseen and expensive crisis, there may not be much flexibility on the part of the financial aid office.

Times Have Changed

Navigating the higher education system is a whole different ball game these days, particularly in terms of cost and complexity. Today's college students are savvier about what they expect to gain for the money they're investing in the college(s) they choose to attend. They have no problem shopping around for a second, or even third, school, especially if the first one they select isn't meeting their expectations or needs.

Students often view their college years as a consumer good in which they have various choices and options just like when they go shopping.

Parents can find it extraordinarily difficult to grasp how much the cumulative cost of higher education could be. The amount of debt that they or their offspring can accrue in just a few years, particularly if the student takes a less traditional approach to college, has changed dramatically. Susan explains that it's an entirely different financial obligation for today's parents than when the parents were college students themselves.

> *"It's not even the same as it was ten or twenty years ago. Sometimes people have absolutely no idea what they're getting themselves or their kids into. There's nothing worse than having to drop out of college with a huge debt load."*

The majority of parents and millennials still agree that financial independence is the ultimate goal after graduation. Unfortunately, even with a college degree, students in their twenties may find themselves caught in a place where they have little money, limited employment opportunities, and student loan payments coming due.

Selecting a college major is another place where generational differences become clear. Many parents had a linear timeline. The expectation was that they would graduate from college, get a job, purchase a home, and perhaps get married and have children. This century's focus on technology and increased digital awareness means career demands are shifting frequently, sometimes too rapidly for colleges to keep up with. There can be a significant gap between what students learn in college and the skills employers and the job market are looking for.

College graduates who can communicate well, think on their feet, tolerate uncertainty, and are willing to risk failure and learn from the experience are highly desirable to today's employers. Given this, students who feel a need to explore and try out multiple occupations/vocations, locations, and even colleges during their late teens and early twenties may actually be more employable when they finally settle down.

Certain twenty-first-century students will be more focused on the end result of the major they choose, such as a job they find meaningful or that they're passionate about, which provides plenty of opportunity for creativity and collaboration. Other students are more interested in the process of college than the finish line. When they graduate they find themselves wondering, "Now what? I have a degree in this subject but where do I go with it? What do I do next?" Still others are unwilling to accept an entry-level job after graduation because they anticipated that a diploma would entitle them to a position that was crafted to their needs and desires.

Parents tend to gravitate more toward majors they hope will be a stepping stone that will guarantee their son or daughter upwardly mobile employment in a rapidly expanding field like Science, Technology, Engineering, and Math (STEM) careers. The current parental generation arrived at college with the understanding that, upon graduation, they would most likely start at the bottom rung of the career ladder. With hard work and perseverance, they'd work their way up in their initial company or take a new job that offered more opportunity for upward mobility.

Additionally, a lot of parents entered the job market in an economy in which a college degree in the field they majored in usually guaranteed a good job for life. Additionally, a number of employers were willing to offer steady employment to college graduates with a liberal arts degree in any subject. In days past, training programs for employees were also offered by companies that hired new graduates.

This disconnect between the parents' wish to have their child "somewhere doing something productive" for four years, hopefully culminating in a college diploma and secure employment, and their offspring's equally strong desire to have a college education that is a quality experience on all academic and social fronts, can lead to passionate debates. After one semester at college, Sandy's daughter wanted to transfer to a university that would be a better fit for her academic goals and personality. Sandy describes the process their family went through.

> *"The first school my daughter went to was a co-op-oriented school. She felt like all the other kids there were very career-oriented and that they were all on track to go in one direction the minute they got there. She went to college as an undecided major because she wanted to explore lots of different career options. So she felt like she didn't fit in with the other kids. We tried to tell her that, even if they thought they knew what they really wanted to do with their lives, it was likely that they'd change their minds at least once."*

She explains why the co-op program had initially appealed to her and her husband.

> *"Her father and I had thought that a college where the students have to take at least one paid co-op would give her some real, hands-on experience and force her to think more about what she wanted to get out of school. We thought it might help her start to think about a career path. Obviously we were wrong!"*

For Sandy, taking into consideration how much had changed in higher education and the workforce since she herself was in college was helpful. She understood that it might no longer be realistic to simply pick a major that sounds interesting without understanding what a job in that field might look like. However, Sandy also looked back on her own college years to try to understand why transferring to a less-structured environment until she found a major that worked for her might be the best move for her daughter in the long run.

> *"I really do believe that college should be a place to explore without pressure. I remember in college I didn't know what I wanted to do either,"* she says.

As to the state of higher education today, Sandy concludes,

> *"I think we need to understand how crazy it is to expect seventeen and eighteen year olds to make decisions that will impact their entire life. This creates a real dichotomy though because, as a parent, it's hard to encourage career and major explorations at the cost of fifty grand a year!"*

This view is one shared by other parents and educators. In the past, trial and error during the college years was tolerated, sometimes even actively encouraged. These days the stakes involved in getting a college degree have never been higher in terms of both cost and competition to get into a four-year college.

Given this, students' more expansive views of college education, combined with the fact that they're often unwilling to settle for an education where they are simply surviving rather than thriving, may indicate that college students are better aligned with today's society than the adults in their lives.

Reaching an understanding with all these divergent views of and approaches to a college education requires strong communication skills and a willingness to listen on everyone's part.

Independence Day

Parents of college-age students may not be familiar with the Family Education Rights and Privacy Act (FERPA), which clearly states that academic or medical information can't be released to parents without student permission (signed waiver) once the student has turned eighteen. This can seem like an unnecessary barrier to concerned parents who may feel "If I'd only known" or "If someone had just shared their concerns."

No longer having immediate access to a student's grades or health reports can also lead to a false sense of security, with parents thinking, "Someone would contact us if something was really wrong, wouldn't they?" On the other hand, FERPA also offers the opportunity for parents and teens to move their conversations to a new, more adult level and may give students more leeway to try to handle things on their own before involving their parents.

Mothers and fathers may not always realize how much their opinion and their continued support still matter to their college-age offspring. Unfortunately, when students defer to their parents' wishes, they may not end up in the place where they want to be. Kasey notes,

> *"What your parents have to say is important and I know mine didn't want me to have any regrets later about not trying to go away to school. But I really didn't want to leave my hometown. I should have put my foot down right from the beginning and said I wanted to go to a college there but it was too hard. As kids we're taught to obey our parents and not question what they say and it's hard not to listen to them when they're footing the bill."*

What students choose to do with their education may not be what their parents had in mind for them either. However, after several years of living away from home, they usually have a better sense of what's best for them than their parents do. About her choice of majors, Hannah says,

"I sometimes wish I hadn't listened to my mom. Her advice about doing art as a hobby on the side might have been good for some people but not for me. I'm a full-time potter now and I'm doing well. I sell my work at many locations and I teach pottery at a school."

To parents, keeping their opinions to themselves and stepping back from the situation may feel like they're not being a good parent. In reality the exact opposite is true. Young people are often more resourceful and resilient than mothers and fathers realize. Planning for their own future builds confidence in their ability to do things on their own without adult help.

One of the less quantifiable goals of a college education is to help students gain and internalize the self-assurance to navigate their educational and career paths independently. Though it takes a little time (and a lot of practice), this attribute is retained by college graduates for years after they leave the college campus and can be applied to many of their future life situations.

More Parent Tips

- Support your son or daughter when they ask you to but don't be a "helicopter" parent or an enabler.
- Make sure they read all the transfer materials carefully and realize what's involved in the college transfer process. Ask if they understand the deadlines, what's being said, and what's expected of them. Remember, no matter how grown up they seem, it's still easy for kids to misinterpret things.
- It's best if they talk to real human beings on the phone or in person rather than relying on the computer, texting, or faxing to communicate. Important paperwork can easily fall through the cracks or get lost.
- Advise them to do things associated with their transfer sooner rather than later. Something will always come up and it's better to leave some wiggle room.
- Give them the chance to succeed or fail in their decision. Some of the most successful people today are those who have tried and failed multiple times, all the while learning valuable lessons from their experience.

7

SEEKING ADDITIONAL PERSPECTIVES

SMART USE OF TECHNOLOGY

Technology can either help or hurt students in the transfer process depending on how it is used. The choice of websites alone is overwhelming. Typing the words "college transfer" into the Google search engine yields over 680 million sites to visit! Some of these sites lead potential transfers to out-of-date information, biased information, or information on products for purchase.

Several of the sites that search engines highlight lead students to sites sponsored by profit or online universities. In general, these do not have a good track record in graduating students. Other sites ask for personal information that it may not be wise to provide.

Reputable Resources

Two college search sites that already have students' personal information because of standardized testing are www.collegeboard.org (SAT) or www.act.org (ACT). In addition, there is a trustworthy government-maintained site called College Navigator (www.nces.ed.gov/college navigator/) that has up-to-date statistics about each college, including the academic majors, sports, and clubs that are available.

Comparing data about colleges on the same page can be useful when students are researching colleges. The www.collegeresults.org site sponsored by the Education Trust can help undergraduates compare universities by graduation rates, admissions data, college endowment, and average net price.

The federal Department of Education sponsors the site https:// collegescorecard.ed.gov that allows a search for colleges by location and major resulting in a colorful, graphic comparison of several colleges. Athletes that are looking to transfer can find useful information on the NCAA website www.ncaa.org if they want to continue competing in their sport.

In terms of college rankings and college preparation, transfers may want to check on search engines provided by *U.S. News & World Report* (www.usnews.com/education), Princeton Review (www.princeton review.com), or the Fiske Guide to Colleges (www.fiskeguide.com). The Fiske Guide continues to be popular among high school students and potential transfers because it gives insight into the culture of the college based upon student interviews.

The Washington Monthly College Guide (http://washington monthly.com/college-guide/) can give the potential transfer hard-to-find information like the number of students who do community service and the number of students who go on to attain a graduate degree. This site is interactive so that one can choose to rank colleges based on things like graduation rates or research dollars. The site, www .educationplanner.org, can help anyone plan the college search and visit process. All of these sites are reputable college search sites useful to transfer students.

What Students Say

Technology can help students get a baseline of information on schools they're considering transferring to. After assembling a list of colleges of interest, the student should go to each college website for more specific information. Keep in mind that these websites are not always objective, especially in terms of the weather. Northeastern college websites often have an abundance of beautiful fall foliage and little evidence of snow.

Many of the sites have an interactive map, allowing visitors to get some sense of the campus layout and types of buildings there. Some college websites offer a virtual tour that can be very helpful if the college is too far away to visit. This does not take the place of an on-site visit because universities tend to highlight the newest and most impressive buildings and facilities.

Instagram photos of colleges at www.instagram.com give an interesting perspective on college life and facilities, especially when comparing what the college posts with informal photos tagged by students.

Potential transfers should check out what each college has to offer them in terms of interesting classes. Many colleges have their course catalogues available online, which makes this research easier. It is important for students to check on class requirements for their intended major as well.

Student reviews of campuses found on www.unigo.com and www.collegeconfidential.com may be interesting, but can also be misleading because readers don't know what types of students have written about the college. This also applies to www.ratemyprofessor.com. The site can give some useful information about the professor's class, but also may involve bias. Happy students are less likely to post and classes that are easier may be rated highly, but that doesn't mean that students learn more in them.

Clubs and activities are also important to evaluate because they change annually, depending on the current student body. Many clubs will have a web page. If no meetings or events have posted in the last two years, the club may not still be active.

Financial Issues

Credit transfer is a huge issue in college transfer. There is one website that can help students figure out which of their credits are likely to transfer (www.collegetransfer.net). Unfortunately, the site does not include every college of interest. It is also important to check this collected information with data from the actual college considered because policies change at individual colleges more frequently than the site can be updated.

Transfers sometimes scramble to pull together a financial package that is workable for them. There is generally less funding available for transfer students than for freshmen. Students can have outside scholarship opportunities emailed to them by signing up with www.fastweb.com. They can also search for scholarships tailored to them on www.scholarships.org. My College Guide is an online blog that also aggregates a lot of useful information about scholarships and financial aid.

Some states have funding opportunities available for their state residents. Students should visit the Department of Education website in their own state. Individual university websites may have transfer scholarships posted on a transfer page. This is not always true, so it pays to ask a financial aid officer if there are any special scholarships for transfers.

Other Online Resources

Students often ask about the best phone apps to use in their college search. The apps that consistently work have larger organizations behind them. These include *Peterson's College Guide for Phones* and the *ACT College Search Apps.*

College newspapers can provide students with timely and interesting information about campus life. Many of these are now available on college websites. Another way to access individual college newspapers is to follow them on Twitter (www.twitter.com). These newspapers will give transfers some sense of the issues on campus and also the quality of student writing for those papers. The standard of writing may interest the student who is planning to major in journalism or creative writing.

YouTube videos are interesting because they give the viewer a glimpse of events on campus and what the college is known for. YouTube videos can also be a good way to get a sense of creative activities (for example, art shows or dance group performances) on campus, both formal and informal. Videos of controversial issues on campus such as racial incidents or free speech concerns may also be worth checking out.

Twitter can be helpful in researching colleges if the student follows college admissions offices. Blogs or weblogs are also a great source of information. Some college websites feature student blogs that reflect the campus culture. Often students decide to "friend" a college on Facebook. It can also be a way to connect with members of one specific class (for example, Boston College Facebook Page for the Class of 2019). This page can allow students to connect with alums following graduation when friends may be living far apart. The Instagram photo app works in concert with Facebook.

Facebook can be both a help and a hindrance. It is a great window on current activities on campus. Just remember, the college can also look at photos and posts of whoever has friended them. A potential transfer may not want the college to see his or her party photos while trying to portray him- or herself as a serious student.

Technology offers tremendous research tools to the transfer student. Technology really can't replace a campus visit because each student is seeing the campus through a filter (what the college has chosen to share). Students should always evaluate the source of information delivered by these ever-changing tools for current relevance and bias.

ADVICE FROM COLLEGE CONSULTANTS

In some cases, boarding school college counselors will help their alums with transfer but public school counselors generally have such a huge caseload that they don't have time to help. At this point families may turn to independent college counselors who work solely for the family rather than for any particular institution.

Having worked with transfers independently for years, the issue of "college fit" has come up in my office repeatedly. Sometimes students don't fit in because the reality of the college was a lot different than they thought it would be. In other cases, the student has just outgrown the college and needs to transfer in order to progress.

> "Students make choices about college as they themselves are changing rapidly. A college that was a perfect fit for an eighteen year old may not fit them at all a few years later when they have matured," states Mark Sklarow the Executive Director of IECA (Independent Educational Consultants Association).

I have found that parents will make the initial call for help with a transfer but after that the work is primarily with the student. Because transfers come in many varieties, there are a few areas where parents remain involved.

TIMES WHEN SUPPORTIVE PARENTS ARE KEY

Students who have mental health issues usually have parents who continue to connect with the counselor. In some cases, the family had worked with the counselor in the initial selection but sometimes it is a new relationship. These parents were hopeful that college would be a positive experience for their son or daughter. In my experience, issues that began in high school can actually be amplified in college because of the stress of living independently, challenging academics, and an underdeveloped support network.

Stress can arise when students arrive home from college and suddenly announce that they are not going back. Parents reach out for help from college counselors because the depression and acting out behaviors that can stem from adult children living at home without structure or purpose can quickly become intolerable. The student may have failed out and will need to address how and why that happened. As Imy Wax (author and consultant from Illinois) says,

> *"You don't want to repeat a failed process. There has to be a reality check with families that there is a thought process involved [in transferring]."*

Locating resources for dealing with addiction or undiagnosed learning difference issues is key. A student who has failed out or withdrawn may need an intermediate step of work or community college classes prior to a transfer. This step can help build the student up both emotionally and academically so that he or she can enter the next four-year college experience with confidence.

> *"The stakes are higher in college transfer because the student has already had one experience that didn't work out so they must be emotionally stable as they begin their new college experience," says Jeff Levy (a California consultant).*

It is important that families understand that sometimes reflection and growth are needed prior to jumping into the next college experience. Some students can strengthen a weak transfer application by showing that they can do well in college classes where they are not enrolled. I tell students that college work is more important in the transfer process than high school work. However, many colleges will look back to the high school record of sophomore transfers (including test scores). If this is a concern, students can apply to those colleges that don't look back to high school.

Tips for Transferring After a Difficult Experience

- Take time to reflect on what worked and what didn't work.
- Stay active either by working, volunteering, or taking classes.
- Get counseling if you continue to be upset or depressed.

Families often need to stay involved when it comes to the financial decision making. Jeff Levy (a California consultant) advises,

> *"Families need to be in communication both with the financial aid office and the registrar because the financial picture is more complex than with high school admissions. They need to figure the credit transfer numbers into the total cost of attendance at the new university."*

Ideally, parents should balance fostering independence in their child while remaining supportive. Here are some questions that parents can ask themselves to decide if they are maintaining that balance.

- Am I trying to run the process and give answers for my child in the process?
- Am I more worried about what the neighbors will say than about the educational experience that fits?
- Do I want a guarantee that the next experience will work out? Is this realistic?
- Am I willing to share my child's psych evaluation and all other relevant materials with the counselor who is trying to help me?

Answering yes to several of these questions indicates that parents are very anxious and may be tipping the balance toward too much control.

Students Can Navigate Straightforward Paths

Some transfer students need little parental involvement because they have gained maturity and focus in their initial college experience. As high school students, they may have wanted something totally different from their home environment but then found that a huge university was too impersonal and hard to navigate. Alternatively, they may have longed for the personal touch of a small college but then realized that they had outgrown the college that was originally a good fit.

Students need to clearly explain why they want to transfer. If they are too "fuzzy" about this, we have found that they sometimes need assistance in differentiating between their current college and their desired college. This involves researching (on college websites) what the new college has to offer versus their current school. The tone of that explanation can be key to admission. Students should explain the reason why they left their prior school with a respectful tone that does not come across as complaining.

General Transfer Admission Tips

- Keep your grades up (don't stop working)
- Stay involved on your current campus
- Don't make your friends feel bad about remaining
- Research transfer choices
- Apply to more than one school
- Visit the campuses

Transferring due to a change in major is fairly common and straightforward, although the family still needs to be aware of the financial effects of the transfer. For example, the student may have taken a computer science class that included one section on cybersecurity that was so interesting that the student decides to major in it, though that major is only offered at a few schools.

Students may want to transfer to a more affordable school, which is often an in-state choice. This can happen because of family trauma or other unforeseen financial difficulties. It can also occur when a scholarship runs out. Some college scholarships only last for the freshman year.

Credit Transfer

Evaluating credit transfer toward graduation requirements is also an important piece of the puzzle of finding a more affordable college. The transfer may not save a lot of money if too many credits are lost. Connecting with the transfer office is an important part of the process.

> *"Make sure you know what will and will not be transferable and don't be afraid to argue over transfer credits once you're admitted,"* advises Nancy Griesmer (Washington Examiner *columnist and consultant). "You may have to present documentation, but it may be worth it if you want to graduate on time. Be prepared to take summer classes also."*

Figuring out the total cost of transfer is complex. Families need to evaluate scholarships not transferable from the prior school, financial aid packages, and credit transfer to gain some sense of the total cost.

> *"It is not only a question of whether credits transferred,"* says Dr. Steve Antonoff. (consultant and author from Colorado). *"Families should notice whether all credits are placed in the electives area or whether they are actually accepted to meet requirements for graduation."*

Trading Up

The siren call of "the dream school" may continue to appeal to some students even after they have spent a year or two at their current college. Their counselor can help them see if that is realistic because colleges with very high retention rates of 95 percent and above take almost no transfers.

Hank Ewert (former boarding school counselor, current Austin College admissions officer) states,

> *"Transfer statistics can alter significantly from year to year. Colleges may go outside published ranges with transfers depending upon the year. Many may not understand that transfer students meet an institutional need, filling empty spaces in a class."*

Very selective colleges will take only a few transfers in a given year. Sometimes they will not have room for any transfers. "Great Books" colleges have a very set curriculum that is not easy to transfer into. These types of colleges may require students to enter as freshmen.

Potential Transfer Pitfalls to Avoid

College counselors highly recommend that potential transfer students think through why they want to transfer because this is a key piece of the transfer application. Counselors have found the following situations to be problematic for students hoping to transfer:

- Obtaining bad grades after the first semester in college (D or lower)
- Looking to transfer when they have only been in college for a few months or less
- Following a boyfriend or girlfriend to the second college
- Blaming professors or other students for their problems
- Trying to get into a college that has a mid-year freshman class
- Misunderstanding the types of classes prerequisite for a new major at the new college

Do You Know What You Want to Do?

Some transfers are simply unhappy and find that they are having a hard time finding friends or clubs that they are interested in.

> *"Applying for a transfer can be an escape valve for a student that is dealing with some issues. Just to know that they can transfer is a relief even if they don't end up doing so in the end," states Ann Montgomery (consultant from Texas).*

Sometimes unhappiness means that the student is not fully engaged with the college because they are tied to a boyfriend or girlfriend at home. Limiting texting with friends at home and trying to live "in the moment" can give a student a new view of the campus. We advise students to try out activities they may not have thought of before they totally give up on the school.

Nancy Griesmer comments, "Once [my student] truly engaged with her college community, neither the idea of transferring nor the boyfriend looked all that good!"

Texting can allow a student an instantaneous connection to friends and family unthinkable ten years ago. Parents may get a message that the student wants to transfer a few weeks into the college year. Their discontent can stem from *"unspoken homesickness and a phone tether to home,"* comments Lori-Potts Dupre (consultant from Maryland). College counselors generally advise against a transfer at this point. Most students have probably not engaged with the new environment enough to know whether they will like it or not and they will have wasted tuition money without receiving any college credits.

When a student is ready to transfer, he or she can hurt him- or herself by disconnecting too abruptly from the current college and failing to work hard academically. As Ann Montgomery says, *"If you don't like the college you are in, don't stop working."*

Students suffering from an undefined malaise can be some of the most difficult for counselors to help.

Imy Wax says that students come to her who "Can't define what they didn't like about the current school except they didn't like the vibe. To make matters worse they may not be able to define what they want in a new school."

These students' self-knowledge and maturity seem to be lacking. Dr. Steve Antonoff describes this problem succinctly.

"Students may have portable problems that will recur at the new college. This dissatisfaction could be related to having difficulty making friends, not being interested in academics, or even expecting everything to be absolutely perfect without any struggle."

Types of Students Who Need More Maturity and Self-Knowledge for a Successful Transfer

- Those who are expecting the change of colleges to fix all problems
- Students who have been unhappy in high school and may have continuing problems like difficulty in making friends

- Shy or very introverted students who may lack the ability to insert themselves into a new social environment
- Students who either can't or won't tell you why they want to transfer
- Students who are already talking about how the second college may not work out

UNDERSTANDING HOW COLLEGES VIEW TRANSFER STUDENTS

Transfers play a specific role in college admissions. As Hank Ewert (Austin College Admissions) puts it, *"Transfers meet an institutional need filling empty spaces."* Freshman enrollment estimates can vary radically from year to year. Missed admissions targets resulting in empty beds can put a financial strain on a college.

That is why colleges have developed various strategies to deal with lower than expected freshman attendance. Long wait lists, spring enrollment, and transfer student enrollment help colleges attain the desired student body size. In the experience of Shelly Levine (college consultant from Maryland), *"It is more difficult for students to transfer into a college that already admits a group of freshmen in the spring that fills a portion of their openings."*

Empty admissions slots may also be due to medical leaves, study abroad, transfer out, or dropping out. There are now more options than ever for students to spend time away from campus. Internships during the school year are definitely on the rise. More students are also taking time away from campus to study abroad or take a gap year doing something completely different. All of these campus "comings and goings" make it very hard for colleges to plan for registration in classes and lodging in college housing.

For many colleges, transfers are full-pay or close to full-pay, which increases the financial stability of the college. This may be true even for colleges that are generous with their financial aid for freshmen. Colleges are not surveyed by ranking services for their transfer financial aid practices. This means that the average package for freshmen may vary widely from the transfer financial aid package.

Universities may also have open slots in certain colleges or majors that they wish to fill with transfers. They can't shift professors from year to year so they will enroll transfer students in order to achieve a better balance of resources leading to more ideal class sizes and accessible professors. Engineering majors are generally the most likely to change major, leaving open spaces to be filled.

Of course the admissions view of transfers is not the complete story. Several faculty members have said that transfers add richness to classroom discussion because of their varied experiences in another college setting. Transfers can also make classes at smaller colleges feel a bit larger and more dynamic because they don't know everyone already and don't make automatic assumptions based upon freshman experiences.

Transfers contribute to social life as well. They bring a fresh infusion of life to campus, especially a small campus. Students that are afraid they will be bored by seeing the same people all the time at events will have new students to interact with. The presence of transfers can also broaden the social scene because they are likely to have developed diverse interests beyond the usual freshman mixer. New club ideas may germinate with the addition of transfers who enjoyed activities like playing the "Game of Thrones" board game or building drones at their former campus.

Many colleges welcome transfers for the diversity they bring to campus as well as the financial support. There are some exceptions. Colleges that follow a very set curriculum such as a "Great Books" curriculum may require that students start over because their prior classes will not be equivalent and therefore won't transfer.

Highly selective institutions that take very few transfers or none at all in a given year may not have transfer-specific services or programs because they have very few students that would use them. They are not set up to specifically help transfers and so transfers will have to be more proactive in getting help with things like housing and advising.

International Students

The number of foreign students on U.S. campuses has been increasing. They contribute to universities both financially and culturally. Foreign transfer students often pay full tuition, which helps the college's financial situation. Colleges that wish to attract a larger international population offer special scholarships to international transfers because of the cultural richness that they bring to campus. International student groups enhance the campus social atmosphere by sharing the food, music, and dance of their culture to the benefit of the entire student body.

Transfers have a positive effect on colleges and universities. They help campuses deal with a constant flux of students as well as adding variety to the classroom and the social structure.

8

ADJUSTING TO A NEW COLLEGE

WHAT STUDENTS THINK ABOUT COLLEGE TRANSFER

No two transfer students are the same. Transfers arrive on their new campus with a variety of (sometimes conflicting) feelings and emotions. This makes it especially crucial for college professionals, parents, and the students themselves to understand that getting accustomed to a different college environment usually won't occur overnight or automatically. In fact, a successful adjustment requires students to show initiative, seek out extracurricular activities, and establish some level of connection with college faculty or staff at their new school.

This chapter shares student perspectives on transfer and the transfer orientation they received, along with adjustment tips from college professionals and some of the "best practices" from universities.

For some students, transferring colleges has a negative connotation. An inner belief that kids who transfer are socially awkward and not able to fit into a college environment can lead to feelings of shame and low self-worth in potential transfers. Transfers who see themselves as being inadequate or failing in some way because they weren't happy at their first college or university frequently feel isolated from their peers who they see as "normal" college students.

Erica, who transferred primarily for academic reasons, advises adopting a different mindset.

"Don't be shy or nervous or feel like a failure because the college you chose first wasn't a good fit for you. It takes a lot of courage to admit

that you don't want to stay there but you need to remember that college isn't a race. Lots of students my age (and their parents) think you need to follow a specific timeline the minute you leave high school. That's a lot of pressure and it's not realistic to think that you'll know exactly what you want to do for the rest of your life."

For students who had a poor academic or social history at their first school, transfer can also be a corrective experience, a second chance. It's not about failure, they say, it's about learning from your mistakes and moving on.

Other college students view transfer as a commonplace, clear-cut transition that will work to their benefit in both the short and long run. According to Jon, who transferred from a Massachusetts college to a major university in New York State,

"If you want to transfer, go for it. There's nothing to be ashamed of or afraid of. It's a perfectly normal thing to do. Lots of people do it!"

Students may need to go through the transfer process themselves to realize that there are numerous reasons to leave a college. A change in their field of study, their financial situation, the ethnic/cultural/racial or religious atmosphere of the college, or their health might prompt a student to initiate transfer.

College transfer can be a positive move, based on personal growth or increased maturity. These students are frequently seeking a more challenging or stimulating environment when they transfer schools. Shanna left her first college to pursue a different career path and to connect with a new group of students. Things turned out exactly as she had hoped.

"It's a great school! I like the program and the people here much better than at my old school which felt really 'cliquey,' like high school. People here are more intelligent. They push themselves academically and choose challenging careers. I like the smaller class sizes too and the fact that you get to know your professors much better than I ever did at my first school."

Daniel found some of the students and his new program of study at the large university he transferred to challenging at times. But there were lots of positive aspects that came with his transfer as well.

"At this university I've been exposed to all sorts of foods, cultures, and music that I'd never experienced before. I dug this diversity after Minnesota. At one music jam there was a bass player from Columbia, a drummer from Japan, a singer from Costa Rica, and me, a piano player from Iowa!"

Piyush, who transferred from a university in India, adds,

"The main reason I wanted to transfer was to get a different type of educational background, to try something new in my college life. I'd been living in India for nineteen years."

Regardless of how college students feel about transfer, one thing they agree on is that being with other transfers or those "in the same boat" is important to them. This is where a well-thought-out and sensitively run transfer orientation at their new college can be exceedingly helpful.

PROS AND CONS OF TRANSFER ORIENTATION

Transfer students gave mixed reviews on the transfer orientations they received. The general consensus seemed to be that the more transfer students the college accepted, the more effort they put into making them feel welcome and appreciated.

The biggest focal point for transfer dissatisfaction was when the college or university required them to attend orientation with the newly arriving freshman class. Transfers unequivocally agreed that they felt like they were entering their new school at a very different maturity level than the recent high school graduates. Freshmen tended to focus on fitting in with other students rather than having meaningful conversations about important campus issues, like race and gender, which was frustrating for the transfer students.

Transfers also noted that the majority of the orientation leaders were young themselves and needed more (or better) training in how to create safe spaces for discussions and how to deal with specific issues that new students arrived on campus with.

Frequently expressed complaints about transfer orientations were:

- They were boring or lame and felt rehearsed and mechanical. Transfers said they could predict what the person running it was going to say before they said it.
- Transfer students left the orientation feeling like no one cared about them and that the college wasn't concerned about their specific needs as transfer students.
- The organizers did a poor job of orienting the transfers to their new campus so they had trouble finding essential buildings like classrooms, the dining hall(s), and the library when classes started.
- The orientation provided a lot of written material in folders about where to get help if they needed it but didn't mention the types of situations that transfers could expect to encounter on their new campus.

The most positive orientation experiences were directly linked to not having to share them with college freshmen who the transfers described as being "in a whole different universe" or "too bright-eyed and bushy tailed."

However, the news wasn't all bad! Brittney has positive memories of her orientation, which made her feel welcome right from the start.

> "At my new school it was mandatory for transfers to attend orientation. It was a one-day thing, to let us meet other transfer students and the professors in our department. First we were all together and then we were divided up by our majors so we could meet each other and see some familiar faces on campus when we started school in the fall. They answered any and all of our questions. We got to sign up for classes too. Doing all this in May helped me prepare for the transition in the fall."

Transfer orientations that the students found helpful shared these characteristics:

- Gave transfers the opportunity to meet with professors and students in their major to ensure their credits were in order and that they knew a few people before the semester began.

- Assigned each transfer a student mentor (someone who transferred themselves was a bonus).
- Offered an informal transfer group that met every couple of weeks for a semester or longer.
- Featured a speaker who discussed what the college could specifically offer transfer students.
- Provided a campus tour that pointed out the buildings transfers would want to find in their first weeks on campus and a fact sheet about where to go for different things they might need.

Transfer students were surprisingly positive about organized activities like icebreaker games, skits, and other activities designed to get them talking to each other. Many transfers also said that having a well-planned transfer orientation helped them build strong connections with other transfer students that lasted at least until graduation and sometimes much longer.

International Transfer Orientation

International transfers tended to get a little extra orienting, which usually focused on showing them how they could:

- Get the most out of their new college, personally and academically.
- Gain an understanding of American laws, which may be different than their home countries', especially in regard to safety requirements or alcohol use.
- Acquire information about where to get help with their English, using U.S. currency, any documentation issues, tuition payments, employment, and credit transfer.
- Learn more about American culture or college groups specifically for them like International Student Associations.

And other essentials like:

- How to get to a local bank and set up an account.
- Where to catch the campus bus to get to local stores.
- How to choose a major (and a minor or double major).

The First Weeks for Transfers

A good start to the school year is very important for transfers' engagement with their new college. Universities are starting to put more thought into orienting transfers to their campus, whereas they used to just assume that transfers would figure things out on their own.

Schools that have developed a group of transfer peer advisors have found that this is a great way to more fully engage with new transfers, especially for social adjustment. Transfer seminars also aid transfers in understanding why their newly adopted college does things the way they do. Best transfer practices for the beginning of the year include:

- Peer ambassadors or upperclassmen assigned to help transfers adjust.
- Transfer scavenger hunts (with rewards) in which transfers have to collect stamps on a card after talking with resource people on campus like the bursar and the reference librarian.
- Transfer seminars: These may be for credit and help start a dialogue with transfers about characteristics of the new institution.
- Transfer centers: These centers pull together all the administrative services that transfers may need in one location.

ADJUSTMENT TIPS FROM COLLEGE FACULTY AND STAFF

Transfer students may figure that they know how to transition to a new college because they have already attended another school. What they may not realize is that each college is different to adjust to in terms of the campus, programs, policies, and people.

Being an early applicant as a transfer is just as helpful in transfer admissions as in freshman admissions. That way the student won't be shut out of classes and possible financial aid awards. There will also be more time to navigate the credit transfer process, which may involve communicating with the registrar at your old school.

Preparing for the transition to a new campus tends to ease the change. Students who have taken the time to connect with the transfer advisor, visited the campus in person, and researched academic programs, living arrangements, and employment opportunities tend to have a much easier time making the change to a new college environment. Meeting with advisors at the new college fosters that relationship so that students feel more comfortable asking for help with things like finding internships.

Fitting In

College advisors that were interviewed tend to agree that fitting in is a huge issue for transfers. Laura Kritikos (coordinator for New Student Programs, DePaul University) describes the transfer socialization process:

> "I tell them it is like entering a group mid-conversation. It can feel like butting in because students already have a set group of friends and organizations may not be looking for new members. This is even more challenging if they don't transfer in the fall. I say 'Brace yourself and jump in!'"

What does it mean to "jump in"? Tracy Mores (University of Wisconsin–Madison Transfer Transition Program) recommends that students ask themselves the following questions concerning activities:

- What do I want to try?
- What activities could I involve myself in that would enhance my intended major?
- What do I want to do after graduation? Could I take advantage of programs, internships, or research that would make that time more successful?

There are many different ways of getting involved on campus. Some are more formal college clubs or organizations and others are more casual. Barnaby Knoll (formerly in Student Services at the University of Puget Sound and Cornell University) says because many transfers live off campus it can be challenging at first to make those casual friendships. He suggests,

> "Activities could be as simple as enjoying athletic events or playing intramurals with friends."

It can be very tempting for transfer students to just stay in their rooms or apartments. Students shouldn't be in a hurry to get home after class. Students are often manning tables for clubs at the student union in the afternoon or sponsoring fun events on campus with free food such as "slacklining" (balancing on webbing between trees) or chocolate chip cookie decorating.

Transfer students have a chance to reinvent themselves and try all new activities at their new school. They are not confined to groups or activities from their old school (with the exception of recruited athletes). Hopefully they have learned to manage their time so that they can get involved in campus life but still stay on top of their classes.

Academic Adjustment

In terms of academics, transfer students often need to hit the ground running. Rapid connection with a faculty advisor in the proposed major is key. Robert Howarth (Cornell University professor and advisor in environmental science) says,

> *"I spend a lot of time talking about different career paths and the importance of internships leading to those careers. It is much easier for the non-transfer students to set up a career related internship because they have had years to think about it, talk to people on campus and apply."*

Sophomore transfers may still be unsure about declaring a major. They should take the time to discuss possible majors with one of their classroom professors in the first semester in addition to getting help zeroing in on a major by talking with staff at the college career center. Certain popular majors at universities, such as engineering, are quite difficult to transfer into and students may need to have a plan B if their initial choice of major doesn't work out. They need to understand the prerequisites in the major they plan to enter and try to get into those classes right away.

Another major that may be difficult to transfer into is education. Several education professors mentioned that their college had very specific education course requirements and they wouldn't accept the credits from other schools toward graduation requirements. This means that the credits would apply as electives and would not help fulfill require-ments in the major.

Different Campus, Different Procedures

A big challenge that students face in adjusting is getting used to the practices and policies at their new institution. Corie Kohlbach (Transfer Services Coordinator at State University New York–Oswego) com-ments,

> *"Many students will start a conversation by saying, "At my previous school we did it differently."*

One of the policies that transfers need to pay particular attention to is the add/drop policy. This policy varies quite a lot from college to college and if the student assumes the wrong deadline they may end up with the dreaded W (or even F) on their transcript.

Timing of class registration can throw some transfer students off track. They are adjusting to a new life on the campus and may not prioritize course registration. Katie Greene (director of Academic Ad-vising at Embry-Riddle Aeronautical University) says,

> *"Students transferring from bigger institutions may get shut out of classes because they are expecting the addition of extra sections."*

Many colleges and universities will not have the flexibility to add a section at the last minute, especially if it is an upper-level course.

A different college calendar can also take some getting used to. Students who switch from a semester system to quarters may have to learn to manage their time differently. Laura Kritikos (New Student Coordinator at DePaul University) notes that students have to adjust to a faster pace of material in the quarter system if they come from a semester-based calendar.

When a student is not adjusting well to a new college environment, college advisors want to know about it. Advisors generally keep an eye on first semester grades, especially if any dip below a C. A number of colleges and universities have developed "early alert" systems so that advisors can be alerted if lots of classes are missed or the student has done poorly on mid-term exams.

Unlike in high school, college students are expected to seek out resources to help them. Dr. Sally Neal (director of Academic Advancement at Ithaca College) has found that transfers may have an internal voice keeping them from seeking help, which goes something like this:

- Everyone here knows something I don't.
- I don't belong here.
- People can tell that I shouldn't be in this college.

This type of inner dialogue is fairly common among transfers especially if the transition isn't as easy as they thought it would be.

Some colleges have transfer seminars to educate students about aspects of the college they may not be aware of. As Dr. Sally Neal (director of Academic Advancement at Ithaca College) puts it, *"Students don't know what they don't know."* Dr. Neal assigns students reading on the value of a liberal arts education in her required transfer seminar. She says,

> *"This helps them answer the question for themselves about why a variety of courses are required."*

The University of Wisconsin has a one-credit optional seminar for transfer students called "The Wisconsin Experience Seminar." In the class the student's goals, values, and skills are assessed. Dimensions of what makes up identity are explored. The students develop a plan as to how they will engage with the university and maximize their use of its resources.

More Tips from the Experts

College advisors, residence advisors, faculty, and new student coordinators offered these suggestions to help students adjust to a new college environment:

- Read your email.
- Go to orientation to meet other transfers and helpful staff.
- Take advantage of a transfer seminar (if offered).
- Try some clubs and activities outside of class.
- Ask for help.

- Try not to make a small problem into a global problem (for example, just because one thing went wrong with a roommate doesn't mean the whole dorm situation is bad).
- Check the basic prerequisites for the courses you are taking. Often an AP class from high school is not enough.
- Go to class regularly and block out time to do the homework.
- If you are having difficulty in a class, get help as soon as possible. This may involve going to office hours, attending review sessions, or finding a tutor.
- Introduce yourself to professors as a new student on campus. This helps professors know who you are and not assume you were there as a freshman.
- Ask yourself, "What do I want to do after graduation and how can the resources here help with that process?"

TRANSFER-FRIENDLY PRACTICES

Colleges and consultants have both been very generous in sharing their transfer-friendly practices. Additionally, many of the college staff who were interviewed were interested in transfer-friendly practices at other institutions in order to improve the experience of their own transfer population.

Financial Practices

Families need to have a discussion about the cost of a transfer. This should include communication with the financial aid office of the prospective college as well. This issue is far more complicated for transfers than for incoming freshmen because they have to weigh the financial aid package along with the credits transferred in order to come up with a true cost.

The credit transfer is very complex on its own because often credits transfer into general electives rather than graduation requirements in the chosen major. The most transfer-friendly financial practices are as follows:

- Financial aid personnel dedicated to working with transfers

- Scholarships that are solely for the transfer population that have reasonable deadlines
- Early credit evaluations prior to acceptance and detailed credit evaluations at the time of acceptance
- Credit granting policies that will allow some credits toward the requirements of a major

Communication Practices

Parents, college staff, and consultants all said that parents are far less involved in the transfer process than they were in the freshman admission process. That doesn't mean that parents aren't interested in what's going on. It is sometimes a challenge for colleges to set boundaries for families so that they feel included but don't impinge on the student's independent choices. Some of the college practices that have fostered better communication with transfer parents are as follows:

- Special transfer parent orientations
- E-newsletters sent out to parents of new students
- Parent portals on college websites
- Facebook groups for transfer parents (monitored, but not formed, by the college)

Academic Practices

Advising transfers on their plan of study is one of the most critical parts of a support system for the transfer population. Institutions that spend some time training their faculty or staff transfer advisors are helping their students make the most of their few years on campus. The most experienced transfer advisors are informed about the best classes for a student to take if they are still exploring different fields. Major advisors should also have some sense of the internships that will be open to transfers who are on a somewhat delayed timeline compared with freshmen.

Colleges are aware that transfer students may fail to get help at the beginning of the school year because they don't know anyone yet and often live off campus. Some colleges have developed an early alert system in which a student's advisor is alerted to reach out to the student if midterm grades were below a C –. Academic practices that are supportive of transfers include:

- Trained transfer advisors and faculty advisors
- Transfer seminars that include an explanation of academic policies, especially add and drop
- Clearly stated major requirements on the website and in print
- An early alert system for students who are having difficulties
- Presence of a Tau Sigma chapter (the National Transfer Honor Society) providing leadership opportunities and scholarships

Residential and Social Practices

Many colleges now host special social events for transfers at the beginning of the year. Transfer clubs or unions have formed at some of the larger universities. Students appreciate the special events the most at the beginning of the term before they get to know more people.

Transfers are a heterogeneous group of people so they often gravitate to more common interest groups as they become more comfortable on campus. Transfer centers are helpful gathering spots for students who may be far enough off campus to feel isolated from other students.

Many transfers plan to live off campus to save money and to maintain a certain independence. Students had mixed feelings about transfer housing on campus. They didn't want to be all grouped together with other students who were unfamiliar with the campus environment. On the other hand, they wanted to have some transfers around who know what they were going through. Some colleges have solved this residential issue by pairing transfers with transfer roommates on halls with students who have been on campus since their freshman year.

Housing and social practices that help transfer students to adjust include:

- Transfer social events such as pizza parties, movie nights, and dinners
- Transfer centers or unions that are social gathering places
- Housing guarantees for transfers, especially in cities where housing is expensive

- Mixed housing for transfers that allows them to engage with both transfers and other upperclassmen

International transfers, first-generation transfers, and military veteran transfers have different needs from the transfer population at large. Many colleges specifically provide special services to these groups within the larger transfer population.

A significant point from these best transfer practices is that transfers should not be lumped in with other new students. Clearly, transfers have more life experience as well as specific advising needs that differentiate them from freshmen. Colleges that provide more individualized financial help, academic advising, and social activities are viewed more favorably by transfers.

9

TRANSFER-TO-TRANSFER ADVICE—
START TO FINISH

BEEN THERE, DONE THAT

These tips from each stage of the transfer process are from real students who have successfully transferred between four-year colleges one or more times. They are both enlightening and useful.

STAY OR GO?

The decision about whether to transfer or not shouldn't be made impulsively or taken lightly. Kyle transferred from a private university in Indiana to a high-ranking public university in Illinois for academic, personal, and financial reasons. Spending some time reflecting and asking himself "Why do I really want to transfer?" was where he chose to begin the process.

> "Be 100% honest with yourself. Feeling like you might have more fun at another college is not a good reason to transfer, but needing to find a college with better classes for your major is. There are certain schools that you know are just for fun so you need to make sure to find one that offers a balance between work and social life," he advises.

Other students offer these suggestions to help potential transfers make their final determination to stay or go:

- Remember that it takes a while for you to fall in love with the first college you go to. Freshman year is a huge life change for everyone.
- Make sure you give your first college enough of a chance before you decide to transfer. You might start liking it a lot after the first year or two.
- Don't have a knee-jerk reaction when things aren't going your way. Sometimes you have to just stick it out rather than trying to run away from your problems by transferring colleges. See if you can make it work before you decide to leave.

EXPLORING OPTIONS

The majority of transfers take the lead in initiating transfer. Parents usually have minimal involvement in the process. Transfer students also tend to handle the application process much differently than they did the first time around. Though applying to a single college can be risky, most students research schools carefully, then apply to an average of one to three colleges or universities, as opposed to submitting seven to ten applications like they might have in high school.

Most transfers agree that investing sufficient time and energy into carefully assessing each college online and in person before applying yields the best results. Here are their other suggestions:

- When you start looking for schools to transfer to, don't limit yourself. Focusing on only one type of school, like liberal arts colleges or schools in big cities, doesn't open your mind to anything new. Make sure your values and goals are aligned with the college(s) you're considering transferring to. This alleviates the likelihood of future problems. If you and the school(s) have the same philosophy about education, they will probably want you to come there as well.
- Be sure to look on the website for the transfer requirements before you apply so you know how you'll match up at the colleges

you're considering. Make sure the academic program and the school are both the right fit for you before you start the transfer process.

- Talk to your advisor, your parents, and the admissions counselor at the college(s) before you commit to applying to them. Reach out to other people who transferred to the schools you're thinking about going to so you can get their feedback.

- It's important to know what you need from a college you're considering transferring to and to make sure the new school will provide you with that. For example, you may need a good advisor who will give you lots of one-on-one attention or a college that offers lots of internship opportunities.

- Don't assume that a public or state school will be cheaper than a private college. Try not to be intimidated by the original price tag of the school. There are lots of ways to make college more affordable like becoming a resident assistant, getting a part-time job, or applying for need- or merit-based scholarships.

ON THE WAY!

Once transfers have a list of colleges, they'll need to start the transfer application process. Eric used his experience at his first college to his advantage when he was writing his transfer application essays.

> *"The second time around my essays were better, more polished, and no longer abstract, because I knew what it was like to be in college and I had very solid reasons why I was transferring. Instead of having to answer the vague concept questions you get when you're applying as a freshman, I was able to write a persuasive essay where I argued why transfer was the best decision for me."*

Other students weigh in on what's important at this stage of the transfer process:

- Once you definitely know you want to transfer, be very thoughtful about your course selection for your last semester at the school you're leaving. Take courses like biology, English, and history.

These will almost always work better for credit transfer than ob-scure electives.

- Don't forget to save your course catalogue and syllabi from your current school. Bring them to your new advisor in case there's a question about whether some of your courses at the previous school should transfer or not.
- Get in touch with the school you're transferring to as often as you want to. Just pick up the phone and call them with any questions. For some things it's much better to talk to a real person.
- Ask if there are any special services for transfer students, like a Facebook page for people in your major or other online or in-person groups where you can ask the students and professors questions.
- Try to find out what extra resources will be available to you before you arrive on campus (like tutoring, health, or counseling cen-ters).

STARTING OVER

Adjusting to life at a new college can be challenging for transfer stu-dents. Not only do they have to acclimate themselves to an entirely different campus layout in a relatively short time, but they also need to get used to new professors and find a group of friends they can relate to. This is particularly true for students who enter a new college in the spring semester when orientation may be minimal. Past transfer stu-dents say, "Be patient, persevere, and forge ahead, even if you encoun-ter unexpected setbacks or obstacles along the way."

Jacquie's first college had not been her top choice and it turned out to be a poor fit for her from the beginning. After taking some time off to work, she transferred to a college that seemed to offer everything she was looking for. However, her roommate never materialized and a few days after she moved in there was a record-breaking snowstorm. Every-thing on campus shut down for two days. Having just arrived at the school, Jacquie had no idea who to turn to. Doubts and fears from her previous college experience threatened to overwhelm her. She recalls,

"All of the bad feelings from my first college came flooding back. But, instead of giving into them, I walked down the street in the snow to the local hospital to see if there was someone I could talk to and there was. He sat with me and talked me through my anxiety until I felt better and went back to campus."

Above all, successful transfers say, "Don't get discouraged or give up. It will be worth it in the end!"

FIRST THINGS FIRST: JOIN UP

Transfer students acknowledged not realizing how important the college atmosphere and "finding their tribe" would be to their well-being when they applied to college as high schoolers. One of the most common concerns voiced by transfer students revolved around making friends and finding a community to belong to at their new college or university.

Though their ways of doing this may have differed, one thing all the transfers who were interviewed agreed on was how important it had been to find ways to get involved in their new campus right from the start. Kyle missed the good friends he had made during his freshman year at his first college so he texted, called, and Skyped them frequently. However, he realized that he was going to have to make an effort to connect at his new school and that the timing of this was key. He notes,

"Once you are there, you have to get out of your room. The first couple of weeks is the most important. There's not too much homework then and people haven't started to get stressed out yet. Don't just sit in your room feeling lonely and sad."

On the other hand, transfers caution other transfer students not to box themselves into friendships the way they might have as less-confident freshmen. "You don't have to stay friends with everyone you meet the first week of school," many of them noted. Neither do transfer students have to limit their friendships to other transfers or students within their major.

Daniel's first impression of his second college compelled him to be strategic in the relationships he formed there.

"It was like a big neighborhood with 35,000 people who all grew up ten miles away from the school! There was this cliquish mentality that I hadn't seen since middle school. I solved this by hanging out with people who weren't in my major when I wanted to relax. We'd do things like go out for tacos and beer. It's what kept me sane."

That's not all Daniel did to acclimate and connect with others. He adds,

"Volunteering for things you're interested in is a good way to meet people too. I volunteered for a school Jazz Festival and got to go for free and meet musicians and other volunteers."

Transfer students stressed that their best relationships were with people they met and got to know through a shared activity. Engaging in sports or favorite hobbies can be reassuring to campus newcomers, along with giving them a place to meet people that have the same interests. Eric found that getting involved in a wide variety of extracurricular pursuits right from the start helped him adjust quickly to his new university.

"I like music and I play the clarinet so I joined the symphony orchestra and a Klezmer band as soon as I got there. I also did some musical theater for a while. Then I became a member of the American Society of Civil Engineers and I was Co-Captain of the Steel Bridge Team. We designed and built a bridge for the regional competition that my college was a part of."

It took Nihar most of his sophomore year to begin to appreciate the social culture of his new university. Once he began to explore what was available, he realized that the sky was the limit.

"As a transfer student, I had to search out clubs, but now I have a mix of campus and non-campus activities and interests. I'm on the Club Tennis Team and a competitive dance team; an Asian-fusion dance group. We've been to Chicago, New Jersey, and California. I'm involved with video production and photography for the university's Sports Network. I also write nonfiction. My book about an Afghanistan cricket team should be out soon!"

Another valuable piece of transfer-to-transfer advice was to try things that they might not have considered before. When Taylor arrived at her new college, the first thing she did was join soccer because she'd played for years. Gradually she stepped out of her comfort zone.

> *"I applied to go on a service trip to Jamaica and it was one of the best things I could have done. And I participated in a 24-hour dance marathon fundraiser for a local camp for families whose lives have been touched by cancer. If you had asked me if I would be interested in doing these things before I transferred, I would have said 'No!' But they were two of the most worthwhile things that I did while I was in college."*

Above all, experienced transfers agree that it's essential to fully commit to the new school. Focus on the positives there rather than looking back at an old school longingly.

FINDING YOUR WAY

Getting used to a new college layout will take time and can be frustrating, especially when it seems like everyone else knows what they're doing and where they're going. Transfers offer these solutions:

- Get to know your campus early on. Spend a day or two just walking around so you get a feel for where your classes will be, where to eat, and where the library is. This is a good way to see how long it will take you to get from one class to another or how far the student union is from your dorm or apartment too.
- Use GPS, Google maps, and your phone to help you locate where important buildings and services are, both on and off campus.
- Ask other students, professors, and staff where things are. This is also a good way to start a conversation that might end in a friendship.

TAKE ADVANTAGE OF TRANSFER EXTRAS

Most transfers freely acknowledged that, even though they'd spent some time in a college setting already, they still needed help on occasion. Many advised new transfers to take part in all the activities that the college puts together before, during, and after transfer, even if they seem trivial or meaningless at first. Nihar took advantage of both online and real-time social activities his new college offered transfers.

> *"I joined several Facebook groups like the Class of 2016 group. There was a Central PA Transfer Picnic the summer before I transferred so I went to that too."*

GET TO WORK!

With the ever-increasing cost of a college education, both domestic and international transfers may find that they'll need some type of employment while earning their degree. There can be long-term social and professional benefits to working too, especially when you're new to a college.

Piyush, an international transfer student, found a job that paid, was personally rewarding, and made a good addition to his resume.

> *"Consider being a resident assistant (RA). When I came to the U.S. I needed a job to help pay my education fees. When I applied for the RA job I had a great interview and got free housing too. It's been really beneficial to me socially. I had to learn to deal with difficult situations. Since I'm not naturally talkative, this was a good thing. I know this is key to my future when I apply to graduate school, go to conferences, or when someone wants to hire me. I think people are more interested in someone who can network and who has good communication and social skills."*

Though they don't have RAs in India, with some research, Piyush discovered that most companies know what RAs are and often prefer hiring them.

> *"As an RA you have to be moral, strict, and show leadership. Even with your friends, the university policies have to be followed. Because of all this, most employers believe that RAs have certain skills that will make them highly successful in the work force,"* he explains.

LEARNING CURVE

A number of transfers mentioned that they felt unprepared for the academic rigor of their new school, which frequently included an increased workload, more competition in their classes, and a greater need to prepare, study, and read materials outside of class.

Professors and other college faculty can be very helpful to transfer students in this respect. Past transfers observe that sometimes it was the unofficial connections they made with faculty that were the most beneficial academically, professionally, and emotionally. They also emphasize that newly transferred students shouldn't feel like the only person they can talk to at their new school is their advisor. They counsel,

- Find a professor to bond with when you first arrive on campus. They don't even have to be in your major if they're interested and supportive.
- Attend your classes. Professors notice if you skip class. They might not take attendance but they will keep it in their heads and it reflects badly on you.
- You may need references for a job or graduate school so try to form good working relationships with professors your first semester at your new college. These professors don't have to be in your field of study. They just need to know you and your abilities.
- If you're assigned to an advisor that isn't helping you, ask for another one or find a professor in your major to assist you. There may be special transfer advisors or transfer centers that can support you too.

Transfers found their advisors to be immensely helpful in certain areas. These included negotiating credit transfer, making sure they were registered for classes in their major in the correct sequence and time frame, and confirming that the student understood graduation requirements. Kasey says her advisor at the third university she transferred to went above and beyond the call of duty.

> *"My advisor looked at everything. Then she went through all the credits my new college didn't want to accept, comparing them with my syllabi from the other two schools I was at previously to show how they really did match their courses. We petitioned their decision*

and I was able to get twelve to sixteen more credits transferred. Then I was still missing a one-credit lab for statistics and she helped me come up with an independent study to get that."

Kasey notes that their relationship continues to be positive, long after graduation.

"I still talk to my advisor (she was also my professor and research advisor). We're Facebook friends and she writes me great references."

FINDING A BALANCE

Students arrive on campus with all sorts of expectations, many of them fueled by the media (or the colleges themselves). At first their new setting may be just as they imagined, with adventures waiting around every bend. Eventually the honeymoon will be over and the reality, that there will be things they like and things that they don't like about college life no matter where they go, will begin to sink in. Regrettably, there is no such thing as a perfect college experience!

Seeing colleges as they really are rather than how they envisioned them often requires a realignment of students' hopes and dreams. Taylor, whose first college was in Washington, DC, clearly recalls the discrepancy between her high school beliefs and the reality of a college student's life in a major urban area.

"I had a picture of college and what it would be like in my mind. Looking back, I guess it was kind of a television version of college where it would be the best place I'd ever lived in. So the whole college experience wasn't really what I had expected."

Gray applied to some of the best American research schools. The first college she attended was a prestigious southern university. Life there was much different than what she had envisioned. She describes the situation she found herself in:

"Unfortunately, I ended up getting exactly what I didn't want when I went to college the first time. I hated the other students from day one. I had always thought college was a socially conscious place but at this

school all the kids were either like camp counselors or just mean. I was depressed, anxious, and angry, lashing out at everyone, which isn't really like me."

Rather than make the best of a difficult situation for four years, she decided to transfer to another top-name college, narrowing her focus this time.

"The second time around I was much more specific about what I wanted in a college, like a good linguistics department and a much smaller college," she recalls.

The second college had its share of ups and downs too. But Gray made many good friends, connected with an unofficial advisor, and found an adult mentor in the Linguistics Department. Currently living in a major northeast city and working on a graduate degree, she concludes,

"I don't regret leaving my first school at all. I know I wouldn't have been as successful as I feel I am now if I had stayed there."

Finding balance can apply to the college to adulthood timeline too. When Jane entered her initial college as a freshman, she had her future mapped out. Things didn't proceed exactly as planned and she found she needed to be more flexible in her approach to her education.

"In high school I had a plan of graduating, going to college, and getting a job—all the normal way—which included four years at one college. Transfer was never part of my plan. . . . Transferring colleges made me a more adaptable person. Not everything will work for you all the time. You may have ideas of how things will be but reality might not always match your preconceived notions. With my transfer I didn't know exactly what would happen but I told myself that it would be ok and that I'd just need to go with it."

Transferring can highlight the fact that all college experiences are not equal. There is a big difference between attending a college where students are disengaged and simply going through the motions to get their credential and one where professors select interesting topics and encourage lively discussions and student enthusiasm and participation levels are high.

Other transfers commented on the necessity of finding a balance between academic and social activities in their new college or university. These needn't be mutually exclusive as both are important to a student's well-being.

Finally, attaining balance includes students taking care of themselves physically as well as mentally. Doing things like getting a good night's sleep, eating regular, balanced meals (rather than existing on Red Bull and ramen!), and exercising regularly all seem obvious. However, in the exhilaration and stress of entering a new college environment, transfer students often let their healthier habits fall by the wayside.

ESPECIALLY FOR INTERNATIONAL STUDENTS

International transfers have multiple adjustments to make: to a second college environment, a brand new culture, and a different language. Though they may seem calm, cool, and collected on the outside, Piyush notes,

> *"It's very daunting to come to live in a place that's so different from your own country."*

Manan still recalls his initial experience at a large American university:

> *"The first day at the university during orientation was a funny experience. I didn't have any cell phone service. I had a lot of luggage and they gave me the wrong keys to the transfer house so I couldn't get in."*

International transfers agree that making American friends who can help you adjust to a new environment, tell you about professors, and teach you the ins and outs of American college life is advantageous.

Communication can be one of the biggest obstacles to connecting with other English-speaking students. Some international transfers said that the majority of their college friends ended up being from their native country because it was so much simpler for them to converse with each other. International transfers observed that the language barrier can have a huge impact on how quickly an international transfer student adjusts to an American university because it can prohibit them from reaching out or talking to U.S. students. Several mentioned how awkward and embarrassing it was to have to keep asking people to repeat what they said or to "slow down."

Though having a roommate who spoke their native language was definitely easier, many international transfers would have preferred an American roommate who could help them increase their fluency in English. International students would also have appreciated it if the International Transfer Orientation at their college had offered them suggestions about safe and supportive places where they could get together and practice their English skills with others.

International students who transfer colleges often have to take extra credits each semester to graduate on time. Forming a good relationship with their professors right from the start made a big difference for them. Most felt their professors understood that they might need some extra help to understand the nuances of the American education system, especially if it was structured differently from their home country's.

The language barrier, combined with academic pressures, can be highly stressful for international transfer students. This can result in a tendency to stick together socially with other transfers who share the same language or social culture. However, international students who made friends from other countries seemed to have the richest experience.

Social and cultural activities may be different than the ones in the student's home country. Previous transfer students noted that U.S. sports were usually a good conversation starter. They suggested international transfers learn about the rules and players beforehand by competing recreationally or on a team, watching them with others, or playing sports-related video games.

For international transfers, joining clubs with an international focus, along with trying out some new American pursuits, seemed to be a winning combination. Many colleges have clubs and organizations that encourage interaction between international and domestic students (often involving food or the arts). Professional clubs with a business or academic focus or those related to their major can also be a good starting point for international transfers. Manan recalls his experience at a large New York university,

"I started a rock band that I was the vocalist for, "Raga & Rock," which plays fusion music with Indian vocals. I also became the chief editor for the Journal for Undergraduate Research *and the president for the Pakistani Student Association (even though I'm not Pakistani!). I was a member of the Academic Integrity Group, which dealt with cases of cheating and misconduct, and a member of the Cricket Club since that's the only sport we know in India! I even started a Transfer Fraternity at the university."*

International students face many of the same challenges that American students find when transitioning between colleges, but their views on transferring seem slightly different. Several mentioned that companies don't only look at a graduate's grades, they also want to know how productively the student spent their college years (for example, professional clubs or organizations, co-ops, or internships). Though they agreed that the social aspects of a campus are just as important as academics, their definition of social seemed to be less on parties and more on what social skills their future employer might be looking for, like the ability to get along with people of all nationalities.

CONCLUSION

Should a student's college years be a time to thrive or merely survive? That's really what it comes down to, isn't it?

College transfer, when approached as one would approach any potentially life-changing decision, can be an invaluable learning experience for young adults. Transfer is less likely to be successful when it's done impulsively or as a way to avoid issues that need to be dealt with before the student can move on to the important business of learning.

Every transfer student's experience is unique. This book shares numerous suggestions from the authors, college faculty and staff, independent college counselors, parents, and transfer students themselves about how to have the most positive transfer possible.

SEVEN TAKEAWAYS FOR READERS

- Put some thought into why transferring would be the best choice. This includes honest self-reflection and taking time to weigh out the pros and cons of transfer.
- Keep the communications lines open. Talking to parents, friends, and education professionals at the current college and the colleges being considered can help students clarify their long-term and short-term goals.
- Take the initiative. A student who wants to transfer to a new college or university should be willing and able to take all the necessary steps

to complete the process. The parents' role should be limited to acting as a sounding board, helping with any financial issues, and accompanying their son or daughter on college visits as a second set of eyes and ears.

- See a gap year as a viable option. Taking a semester or a year off between four-year colleges can be a positive experience as long as it is structured to help a student figure out what he or she wants to do next. Positive gap year experiences can include work, internships or volunteering, classes at a community college, or purposeful travel.
- Utilize all support services offered to transfer students before, during, and after arriving at the new college or university. These can include online or in-person social groups for transfers, transfer orientation, peer mentors, special transfer student seminars, meeting with a transfer advisor, or going to a transfer center.
- Get involved in the new school right from the start. Spend time doing familiar activities, but try new things as well. Connecting with other students and professors will make the adjustment period much easier.
- Don't look back! College transfer doesn't imply a failure on anyone's part. It simply indicates that the first school wasn't a good fit. These days it's important for students to find a college that gives them a well-rounded academic experience, a fulfilling social life, and relevant employment skills, not just a piece of paper.

Life is rarely a static affair. Circumstances change, places change, and relationships change. The only thing people have control over is how they respond and adjust to these changes. The competencies transfer students acquire are not only relevant to the college transfer process, they're also lifelong skills.

Students were able to clearly articulate how they felt the transfer experience set the stage for future transitions. Jane transferred a decade ago but she still hasn't forgotten what she learned from her experience.

"Transferring helped me learn to identify external and internal cues that it might be time for a change. Transferring successfully allowed me to ask later in life 'Is this the right job, city, or relationship?' and assess what was going on with a more critical eye," she says.

Other external skills that transfers gain that can be applied to almost every transition the student will have as an adult include:

- Problem solving
- Decision making
- Ability to prioritize tasks
- Willingness to take risks and to fail
- A sense of commitment to overcome challenges and learn from disappointments

And that's not all! Through the transfer process students often benefit in less apparent ways as well. Some inner strengths students who transferred acquired included:

- Increased awareness through self-reflection
- Resilience and grit
- Flexible mindset and an ability to adapt to new situations
- Being comfortable with ambiguity and uncertainty
- Determination to succeed in their life goals

College transfer can supply students with the foundation that will help them self-direct and navigate how they learn while in college and for the rest of their lives.

APPENDIX A

Key Transfer Terms

Academic Plan

A plan or outline of college courses that a transfer student will need to take over their college career to fulfill specific major, minor, and graduation requirements so they can graduate in a timely and cost-efficient manner.

Accuplacer

The Accuplacer is a computer adaptive test (in which subsequent questions are determined by prior answers) from the College Board. The test results in reading, writing, and math may be used by academic advisors to place a student in courses that match their skill level and give them the best opportunities for success.

Admission Application Fee Waiver for Transfers

Allows transfer students who are eligible for a Pell Grant to waive the college or university's application fee. Other transfers who qualify for this waiver are those who are part of a federal, state, or local program that provides assistance to low-income families or whose family income falls within the guidelines established by the USDA for the free or reduced price lunch program.

Alternative Evaluation/Prior Learning Assessment

Students who have been out of school, in the military, or working for a few years may benefit from this type of evaluation, which grants student educational credit for life experiences and written work in other settings. Some colleges call this a PLA or a Prior Learning Assessment because it includes a review of all work with academic merit up to that point in time.

Application Supplement

A transfer application supplement varies from college to college. It often contains a series of questions about residency or academic interests. Some colleges have more extensive supplements that can include a graded piece of writing, an essay about the reason for transfer, or a portfolio.

Articulation

Articulation is an agreement between colleges as to how credits and classes from one college will transfer to another school. This process of evaluating prior work for credit by comparing courses is usually carried out by the college or university registrar. Two other types of articulation agreements are program articulation agreements (for credits to be applied toward a specific degree) and guaranteed admission agreements.

CollegeFish

An online resource (supported by Phi Theta Kappa, the International Honor Society of Community Colleges) that helps promote seamless and timely transfers between students from two-year colleges and the higher education personnel who work with them.

Core Curriculum

This consists of course requirements, regardless of major, taken by all students at a given college. The number and type of courses varies depending on the college.

Course Equivalencies/Transfer Credit/Transcript Evaluation

Student transcripts are evaluated by college administrators to see how many credits will transfer based upon their prior college's accreditation of the institution, prerequisites, course description, textbook used, method of instruction, perceived rigor, and letter grade. Equivalency acceptance can vary widely among colleges.

Course Sequences

Some college majors require a defined sequence of courses, especially in majors with a lot of requirements like engineering and education. If a transfer has taken a course out of sequence, it can cause problems with both scheduling and prerequisites. They may have to take summer classes to get back on track or even an extra semester or year of college.

Education Gap

A gap in a student's higher education timeline that is more than a summer long will need to be explained to the college.

Extramural Student

A college student who is not enrolled in a degree-granting program but is receiving college credits from a school. These credits may or may not transfer to the college or university that the student ultimately graduates from.

FERPA (Family Educational Rights and Privacy Act of 1974 [Amended in January 2012])

This law defines who has the rights to a student's educational records. Parents have the rights to educational records until the child turns eighteen. The rights transfer to the student beginning on the first day of class following a student's admission to a college or university. After this time the school must obtain the written consent of all present and former students before releasing any personally identifiable data from their records. There are two exceptions to this. The student can sign a waiver of their rights under FERPA, or, if the child can be claimed on the parent's tax return as a dependent and the parent can prove this to the college, they gain rights to view the student's records.

Grade Point Average (GPA) Recalculation

College registrars handle grades from other colleges in a variety of ways. They may remove certain courses from the college GPA calculation or even alter the number of credits received. A student may believe they have a certain GPA when in fact the new school may have calculated a new one.

Guaranteed Transfer

If a student is able to complete one year at another college with a good GPA, defined by the college offering the transfer (usually a 3.0 or above), some colleges will offer a guaranteed transfer to applicants so they don't have to go through the transfer admission process.

Honor Society for Transfers/Tau Sigma

Tau Sigma National Honor Society is designed just for transfer students and currently has over one hundred chapters. Membership provides students with many leadership opportunities and the chance for students who are earning an associate degree and are planning to enroll in a bachelor's degree program to apply for scholarships.

International Transcript Evaluation

International transfer students need to have their transcripts translated into English and evaluated for credit. Companies in good standing for credit evaluation can be accessed from the website of the National Association of Credential Evaluation Services (www.naces.org).

Nonmatriculated Student

Students in this category are either taking classes without being admitted to the college or have left after attending the college for some period of time. These students are not eligible for financial aid or participation in athletics.

Residency (Academic)

This term refers to the amount of time a student has to be on campus taking classes or credits that a transfer student is required to complete at the receiving institution to graduate.

Residency (State)

Determines whether or not the student is a resident of the state the college is in and therefore eligible for in-state tuition or grants.

Rolling Admission

Universities and colleges that offer rolling admission have no unequivocal admission deadlines. The college will evaluate applications as received and return an answer within a set period of time. However, many of the schools do have priority deadlines, which means that later applicants may not get the most desirable housing, financial aid package, or choice of major.

TOEFL (Test of English as a Foreign Language)

This test measures the ability of nonnative English speakers to use and understand the English language as it is heard, spoken, read, and written in the university classroom. There is a similar English language proficiency test called IELTS (International English Language Testing System), which assesses a student's English language skills and his or her ability to study in a setting in which English is the primary language.

Transfer Advisors

Faculty who advise students on all things related to their transfer, including preparing their transfer application, finding financial resources, and connecting transfers with other professors or department heads who can act as mentors.

Transfer Scholarships

Some colleges will have transfer-specific scholarships that are different from those received by freshmen. Transfer scholarships vary by type, amount, and eligibility requirements.

Transfer Student

Each institution has a different definition of what constitutes a transfer student. Some universities consider a student a transfer when he or she has taken one credit after high school while others may not consider him or her a transfer until he or she has completed at least thirty credits.

APPENDIX B

Colleges that Consistently Accept the Most Transfers

What is notable about this list (that excludes online universities) is that it includes the largest state university systems such as Texas, California, and Florida. These campuses admit thousands of transfers every year, so systems are in place to make the process easy (*U.S. News & World Report*, 2014 data).

University of Central Florida	Orlando, FL
California State University–Northridge	Northridge, CA
University of Texas–Arlington	Arlington, TX
Florida International University	Miami, FL
University of Houston	Houston, TX
University of Maryland–College Park	Adelphi, MD
California State University–Fullerton	Fullerton, CA
San Jose State University	San Jose, CA
Texas State University	San Marcos, TX
California State University–Long Beach	Long Beach, CA

University of North Texas	Denton, TX
California State University–Sacramento	Sacramento, CA
University of South Florida	Tampa, FL
Arizona State University–Tempe	Tempe, AZ
San Francisco State University	San Francisco, CA
San Diego State University	San Diego, CA
University of California–Los Angeles	Los Angeles, CA
University of California–Davis	Davis, CA
Portland State University	Portland, OR
California State University–Los Angeles	Los Angeles, CA
Texas Tech University	Lubbock, TX
University of North Carolina–Charlotte	Charlotte, NC
Northern Arizona University	Flagstaff, AZ
Georgia State University	Atlanta, GA
California State University–Dominquez Hills	Carson, CA
California State Polytechnic University	Pomona, CA
Ohio State University–Columbus	Columbus, OH
Temple University	Philadelphia, PA
Texas A&M University–College Station	College Station, TX
Sam Houston State University	Huntsville, TX
CUNY–Queens College	Flushing, NY
George Mason University	Fairfax, VA
University of California–San Diego	La Jolla, CA

Washington State University	Pullman, WA
Florida Atlantic University	Boca Raton, FL
University of Nevada–Las Vegas	Las Vegas, NV
University of Houston–Downtown	Houston, TX
University of Texas–Austin	Austin, TX
Old Dominion University	Norfolk, VA
California State University–San Bernadino	San Bernadino, CA
Virginia Commonwealth University	Richmond, VA
Kennesaw State University	Kennesaw, GA
University of California–Berkeley	Berkeley, CA
Fort Hays State University	Hays, KS
University of Minnesota–Twin Cities	Minneapolis, MN
California State University–East Bay	Hayward, CA
CUNY–Brooklyn College	Brooklyn, NY
Texas A&M International University	Laredo, TX
CUNY–Baruch College	New York, NY
Wayne State University	Detroit, MI
College of Southern Nevada	Las Vegas, NV
Utah Valley University	Orem, UT
University of Arizona	Tucson, AZ
University of California–Irvine	Irvine, CA
University of Texas–San Antonio	San Antonio, TX
Florida State University	Tallahassee, FL
Towson University	Towson, MD
University of Florida	Gainesville, FL
Iowa State University	Ames, IA

CUNY–Hunter College	New York, NY
University of Texas–Dallas	Richardson, TX
California State University–Fresno	Fresno, CA
Dixie State University	Saint George, UT
University of Texas–El Paso	El Paso, TX
Oregon State University	Corvallis, OR

APPENDIX C

Sample of Varying Transfer Policies (by Survey)

PARTICIPATING COLLEGES

- American University
- Arcadia University
- Carnegie Mellon University
- Denison University
- Elizabethtown College
- Goucher College
- Hobart and William Smith College
- Keuka College
- Marist College
- McDaniel College
- Medaille College
- Muskingum University
- Otterbein University
- Rochester Institute of Technology
- SUNY College at Geneseo
- Susquehanna University
- Temple University
- University of Rochester
- Villanova University

WHO IS A TRANSFER?

- *Colleges that consider you a transfer when you have taken any post–high school course as a matriculated student:* American University, Arcadia University, Elizabethtown College, Goucher College, Hobart and William Smith College, Marist College, McDaniel College, Medaille College, Muskingum University.
- *Colleges that consider you a transfer when you have obtained (three to thirty) college credits:* Denison University, Keuka College, Otterbein University, Rochester Institute of Technology, SUNY College at Geneseo, Temple University, University of Rochester, Villanova University.

DOES THE COLLEGE CONSIDER STANDARDIZED TESTING FOR TRANSFERS?

- *Colleges that consider standardized testing for transfers with a low (up to thirty) number of credit hours:* Arcadia University, American University, Carnegie Mellon University, Rochester Institute of Technology, University of Rochester, Villanova University.
- *Colleges that don't consider standardized testing for transfers:* Denison University, Hobart and William Smith Colleges, Goucher College, Keuka College, Marist College, Medaille College, Otterbein University, Temple University.

WHAT GRADE WILL BE ACCEPTED FOR A TRANSFER CREDIT?

- *Colleges that accept transfer credits of C and above:* American University, Denison University, Hobart and William Smith Colleges, Keuka College, McDaniel College, Medaille College, Rochester Institute of Technology, University of Rochester, Villanova University.
- *Colleges that accept transfer credits of C – and above:* Arcadia University, Goucher College, Otterbein University, Susquehanna University, Temple University.

IS THERE GUARANTEED HOUSING FOR TRANSFERS?

- *Colleges with guaranteed housing for transfers:* American University (for transfers with fewer than thirty credits), Arcadia University, Denison University, Elizabethtown College, Keuka College, Hobart and William Smith Colleges, McDaniel College, Medaille College, Muskingum University, SUNY College at Geneseo.

ARE THERE SCHOLARSHIPS SPECIFIC TO TRANSFERS?

- *Colleges with transfer specific scholarships:* American University, Denison University, Elizabethtown College, Goucher College, Hobart and William Smith Colleges, Marist College, McDaniel College, Medaille College, Otterbein University, Rochester Institute of Technology, Susquehanna University, Temple University.

APPENDIX D

College Transfer Timeline (Fall)

- **Early January or before:** Make decision to transfer
- **January or as soon as you decide to transfer:**

    - Finalize college list to apply to
    - Obtain dean's letter of good standing from current college
    - Obtain faculty reference from current college
    - Begin college visits and/or online research

- **January until week prior to transfer deadline:**

    - Request transfer credit review at list of transfer colleges
    - Complete transfer personal statement (Common Application)
    - Complete transfer applications
    - Request official transcripts for transfer colleges to be sent from all prior colleges
    - Request official SAT/ACT scores to be sent (if required)

- **February 1–April 1:** Transfer deadlines for the most selective colleges
- **March 1–June:** Decision received from early group of colleges:

    - Deposit required within a few weeks of decision
    - Notify prior college that you will not be returning

- **April 1–June 30:** Transfer deadlines for many colleges (some have rolling admissions)
- **May 1–summer:** Decision from colleges not on the early timeline:

  - Deposit required within a few weeks of decision
  - Notify prior college that you will not be returning

APPENDIX E

College Transfer Timeline (Spring)

Note: Several colleges do not offer spring transfer/entry.

- **Mid-spring semester–early summer:** Make decision to transfer
- **Spring semester or as soon as you decide to transfer:**

  - Finalize college list to apply to
  - Obtain dean's letter of good standing from current college
  - Obtain faculty reference from current college
  - Begin college visits and/or online research

- **Summer until week prior to transfer deadline:**

  - Request transfer credit review at list of transfer colleges
  - Complete transfer personal statement (Common Application)
  - Complete transfer applications
  - Request official transcripts for transfer colleges to be sent from all prior colleges
  - Request official SAT/ACT scores to be sent (if required)

- **August 1–October 1:** Transfer deadlines for the most selective colleges

- **September 1–December 1:** Decision received from early group of colleges:

    - Deposit required within a few weeks of decision
    - Notify prior college that you will not be returning

- **September 1–December 15:** Transfer deadlines for many colleges (some have rolling admissions)
- **October 1–early January:** Decision from colleges not on the early timeline:

    - Deposit required within a few weeks of decision
    - Notify prior college that you will not be returning

APPENDIX F

College Transfer Resource List

SPECIFICALLY FOR TRANSFERS AND FAMILIES

Academic Resources

- CollegeTransfer.net: Great source on articles for college transfer with topics ranging from majors to undecided students, some organizational tools to help students track progress toward a degree.
- Transferology.com: This site, created and supported by College-Source Inc., helps students determine which of their courses will transfer to specific colleges or universities. It also has a feature that allows students to explore options for summer college classes.

Community College

- "Tips on Transferring from a 2-Year to a 4-Year College," https://bigfuture.collegeboard.org/find-colleges/college-101/tips-on-college-transferring-from-a-2-year-to-a-4-year-college.
- "10 Tips for Transferring from Community College," by Jeremy S. Hyman and Lynn F. Jacobs, http://www.usnews.com/education/blogs/professors-guide/2009/09/16/10-tips-for-transferring-from-community-college.

- "A Third of Students Transfer before Graduating, and Many Head toward Community Colleges," by Jennifer Gonzalez, http://chronicle.com/article/A-Third-of-Students-Transfer/130954/.
- Collegefish: http://www.collegefish.org/transfer-students.

Financial Resources

- Request for Transfer Admission Application Fee Waiver Form for Transfer Students, http://www.nacacnet.org/studentinfo/feewaiver/Documents/TransferWaiverForm.pdf.
- Unigo Scholarship Directory: A directory with scholarships, awards, and grants listed by category including athletic, minority, and merit-based financial assistance, https://www.unigo.com/scholarships#/fromscholarshipexperts.
- Federal Student Aid, U.S. Department of Education, https://studentaid.ed.gov/sa/fafsa/next-steps/student-aid-report.
- *The College Solution: A Guide for Everyone Looking for the Right School at the Right Price*, by Lynn O'Shaughnessy (Pearson Education, Inc., 2012).

Gap Year

- "Gap Year: When Your Teen Doesn't Choose College—A Parent's Perspective," by Susan Henninger, http://www.rocparent.com/parenting/teens/gap-year/.
- "Revisiting Samantha," by Susan Henninger, http://www.rocparent.com/parenting/teens/revisiting-samantha/.
- "How to Have a Successful Gap Year—Tips for Malia Obama and Other High School Grads," by Anya Kamenetz, http://www.npr.org/sections/ed/2016/05/03/476506144/how-to-have-a-successful-gap-year-tips-for-malia-obama-and-other-high-school-gra.
- "Pros and Cons of Gap Year," by Sally Rubenstone, http://www.collegeconfidential.com/dean/000308/.
- *The Gap-Year Advantage: Helping Your Child Benefit from Time Off Before or During College*, by Karl Haigler and Rae Nelson (St. Martin's Press, 2005).

- *The Complete Guide to the Gap Year: The Best Things To Do between High School and Collegem,* by Kristin M. White (Jossey-Bass, 2009).
- *Gap Year: How Delaying College Changes People in Ways the World Needs,* by Joseph O'Shea (Johns Hopkins University Press, 2014).

International Transfer Students

- Tips for International Students Who Attend National College Fairs, http://www.nacacnet.org/college-fairs/students-parents/Pages/Tips-for-International-Students.aspx.
- "5 Application Tips for International College Transfer Students," by Giovana Rodrigues Manfrin, http://www.usnews.com/education/blogs/international-student-counsel/2015/10/13/5-application-tips-for-international-college-transfer-students.
- "5 Things to Consider Before Transferring to a U.S. College," by Yao Lu, http://www.usnews.com/education/blogs/international-student-counsel/2013/12/12/5-things-to-consider-before-transferring-to-a-us-college.

LGBTQ Students

- The Campus Pride Index: National Listing of LGBTQ-Friendly Colleges and Universities, http://campusprideindex.org/.
- *U.S. News & World Report,* "Consider College Options Carefully as a Transgendered Student": Summarizes some key elements transgender students and parents or caregivers should be looking for to find the best college fit for a student, http://www.usnews.com/education/best-colleges/articles/2014/09/18/consider-college-options-carefully-as-atransgender-student.
- The Campus Pride Trans Policy Clearinghouse: A resource for transgender policies at colleges and universities, http://www.campuspride.org/tpc/.

National College Fairs

- "Transfer Students—College Fairs Can Meet Your Needs," http://www.nacacnet.org/college-fairs/studentsparents/transfer/Pages/TransferStudents.aspx.
- "What Questions Should a Potential Transfer Student Prepare to Ask at a National College Fair?" http://www.nacacnet.org/college-fairs/students-parents/transfer/Pages/Transfer-Student-Questions.aspx.

FOR COLLEGE PROFESSIONALS WORKING WITH TRANSFER STUDENTS

- National Institute for the Study of Transfer Students, https://transferinstitute.org/about-us/.
- *Transition and Transformation Playbook*, https://transferinstitute.org/wp-content/uploads/2016/05/Transition-And-Transformation-NISTS-book2.pdf.
- *The Map-2-Transfer Manual: 2016*, by the Commission on Independent Colleges and Universities of New York.
- Recruiting and Retaining Transfer Students Successfully at Four-Year Institutions, http://www.nacacnet.org/research/transfer/KeystoSuccsss/Pages/Recruiting--Retaining-Transfer-Students-Successfully.aspx.
- "Transfer Is Trending," http://www.nacacnet.org/research/transfer/Pages/Transfer-is-Trending.aspx.
- "The President Proposes to Make Community College Free for Responsible Students for 2 Years," https://www.youtube.com/watch?v=d-QDfEMXAgk.

College and University Resources

- College course catalogue from prior college (helps with course equivalencies)
- College website's transfer page
- College registrar's office and webpage (credit transfer)
- College financial aid office and webpage (shows financial aid and scholarships)

- College transfer coordinator
- College admissions officer responsible for transfers

FOR FURTHER READING

College Search Process

- *College Match: A Blueprint for Choosing the Best School for You*, 12th edition, by Dr. Steven Antonoff (Educonsulting Media.com, 2014).
- *Colleges That Change Lives: 40 Schools That Will Change the Way You Think About College*, by Loren Pope (Penguin Books, 2012).
- *Fiske Guide to Colleges*, by Edward Fiske (Sourcebooks, Inc., 2017).
- *The College Handbook* (College Board, 2017).

Education Professionals

- Guided Path professional software.
- Myers-Briggs Type Indicator: A personality test that assesses the way individuals use their perception and judgment, http://www .myersbriggs.org/my-mbti-personality-type/take-the-mbti-instru ment/.

Financial

- "Paying for College Is a Family Affair," http://www.nacacnet.org/ studentinfo/articles/Pages/Paying-for-College-is-a-Family-Affair .aspx.
- *Paying for College Without Going Broke*, by Kalmen A. Chany (Princeton Review, 2017).
- *Getting Financial Aid 2017* (College Board, 2016).
- *The Financial Aid Handbook: Getting the Education You Want for the Price You Can Afford*, by Carol Stack and Ruth Vedvik (The Career Press, Inc., 2011).
- *The Total Money Makeover: A Proven Plan for Financial Fitness*, by Dave Ramsey (Thomas Nelson, Inc., 2013).

International Students

- *International Student Handbook* (College Board, 2017).
- *Succeeding as an International Student in the US and Canada* by Charles Lipson and Allan Goodman (University of Chicago Press, 2013).

Learning Disabilities

- National Center for Learning Disabilities: This organization provides leadership, public awareness, and grants to support research and innovative practices in learning disabilities, http://www.ncld.org/.
- *The K & W Guide to Colleges for Students with Learning Differences*, 13th edition, by Marybeth Kravets and Imy Wax (Princeton Review, 2016).
- *College Success for Students with Learning Disabilities: Strategies and Tips To Make the Most of Your College Experience*, by Cynthia Simpson and Vicky G. Spencer (Prufrock Press, 2009).

Students and Families

- *Barron's Profiles of American Colleges 2016*, or current edition. General statistics from Common Data Set.
- *Don't Tell Me What to Do, Just Send Money*, by Helen Johnson and Christine Schelhas-Miller (St. Martin's-Griffin Press, 2011).
- *Empty Nesters: 101 Stories about Surviving and Thriving when the Kids Leave Home* (Chicken Soup for the Soul Publishing, 2008).
- "Great Jobs, Great Lives: The 2014 Gallup-Purdue Index Report," https://www.luminafoundation.org/files/resources/galluppurdue index-report-2014.pdf.
- *How to Study in College*, by Walter Pauk and Ross Owens (Cengage Learning, 2014).
- *Letting Go: A Parents' Guide to Understanding the College Years*, by Karen Levin Coburn and Madge Lawrence Treeger (Harper Collins, 2016).
- *The Secrets of College Success*, by Lynn F. Jacobs and Jeremy S. Hyman (Jossey-Bass, 2013).

- *There Is Life After College: What Parents and Students Should Know About Navigating School to Prepare for the Jobs of Tomorrow*, by Jeffrey J. Selingo (William Morrow, 2016).
- Wintergreen Orchard House College Admissions Data Sourcebooks (CADS) 2016 (or current edition).

ABOUT THE AUTHORS

Photo by Thomas Hoebbel.

Lucia D. Tyler has worked with many families to help them make the most of the admissions process to find a good college match. The very first student she helped as an independent counselor was a transfer student!

Lucia is a Certified Educational Planner, which requires significant college advising experience in addition to passing a rigorous exam. In order to keep up to date on changing college programs and facilities, she travels to over thirty-five colleges per year. She has evaluated over 285 colleges in twenty-five states. Lucia has presented on various college admissions topics at the national conference of the Independent Educational Consultants Association, as well as giving talks at local libraries. She has also written articles on college admissions for Unigo.com and the *Ithaca Journal*. All of these activities help keep her up to date so that she can help families navigate the ever-changing college admissions process.

Prior to opening her own consulting business, Lucia Tyler worked at the Cornell Veterinary College giving presentations and counseling applicants. She worked in higher education at Cornell University for over fifteen years. Her professional roles included researcher, lecturer, lab manager, student mentor, and curriculum developer. She enjoys reading, singing, swimming, kayaking, skiing, and walking her new rescue dog, Starry. Lucia and her husband, David, have lived in the Ithaca area since they met at Cornell University. They have two grown children.

Photo by One Sharp Joe.

Susan E. Henninger is a freelance writer living in the Finger Lakes Region of Upstate New York. She received her bachelor's degree in social work from Cornell University and a master's degree in social work from Boston University. During her career as a social worker, Sue counseled a broad range of families struggling with various challenging situations.

Sue has three sons, now in their twenties. In their K–12 years she was a tireless volunteer and advocate for them and their schools. During their college years she accompanied each of them on college visits and was a supportive and neutral sounding board through their decision-making processes. As a professional writer, Sue has written hundreds of articles about education and parenting.

When Lucia Tyler approached her about co-authoring a book on college transfer, Sue (a transfer student herself in the 1980s) was intrigued. She delved into the subject and was surprised to discover that, though one out of three college students transfer, there were few resources available to help them and their families. Sue quickly became committed to working with Lucia to develop a step-by-step guide to college transfer that would provide readers with the information and strategies they needed to navigate an often complicated and costly process.

Sue and her husband, Neil, are currently enjoying their empty nest with a Rhodesian Ridgeback rescue dog. She spends her free time camping, boating, traveling, and enjoying time on the lake with friends and family. She's also an avid reader, baker, and hostess. Learn more about Sue at SueHenninger.com.